BUDDHISM
AND
JUNGIAN PSYCHOLOGY

Other Titles From New Falcon Publications

BUDDHISM AND JUNGIAN PSYCHOLOGY

By
J. Marvin Spiegelman, Ph.D.
and
Mokusen Miyuki, Ph.D.

1994
NEW FALCON PUBLICATIONS
TEMPE, ARIZONA, U.S.A.

International Standard Book Number: 1-56184-111-0

Library of Congress Catalog Card Number: 85-70850

First Edition 1985
Second Printing 1987
Third Printing 1994

The paper used in this publication meets the minimum requirements of the American National Standard for Permanence of Paper for Printed Library Materials Z39.48-1984

Address all inquiries to:
NEW FALCON PUBLICATIONS
1739 East Broadway Road Suite 1-277
Tempe, AZ 85822 U.S.A.

(or)
1605 East Charleston Blvd.
Las Vegas, NV 89104 U.S.A.

Table of Contents

ACKNOWLEDGEMENTS

The Authors are appreciative of Falcon Press and the following publishers for re-printing from their publications. Every effort has been made to obtain permission, most of which have been received by press time:

The Eastern Buddhist, The Eastern Buddhist Society Otani University, Kita-ku, Kyoto, Japan for "The Psychodynamics of Buddhist Meditation," October 1977.

Journal of Humanistic Psychology, for "Dying Isagi-Yoku" in Fall 1978.

Journal of Analytical Psychology, London, for "A Jungian Approach to the Pure Land Practice of Nien-fo" in the issue of July 1980.

"The Ideational Content of the Buddha's Enlightenment as Selbstverwirklichung," from *Buddhist and Western Psychology*, edited by Nathan Katz, c 1983. Reprinted with permission from Shambhala Publications, Inc., P.O. Box 308 Back Bay Annex, Boston, MA 02117.

Quadrant, New York, for "Self-realization in the Ten Ox-Herding Pictures" in Spring 1982, and the C.G. Jung, Foundation for Analytical Psychology.

Princeton University Press for quotes from Jung's Collected Works.

"East and West: A Personal Statement," also appeared in Japanese, "Jung Shinrigaku-Higashi to Nashi no Deai" (Jungian Psychology - Encounter of East and West), Shin Yosha Ltd., Tokyo, 1984.

FOREWORD

By J. Marvin Spiegelman

It is close to a quarter century since Jung died and about half a century since he wrote the remarkable essays on eastern religion found in Volume 11 of his collected works, *Psychology and Religion: West and East*. A present reader can only be dumbfounded by the perspicacity and perception demonstrated by Jung in his commentaries on Tibetan Buddhism, India and Yoga, Chinese Taoism as revealed in the *I Ching*, Eastern meditation, and Zen Buddhism. He not only understands what, for most western people, were opaque and rare religious experiences, but he also brings them into relationship with western perspectives of both a similar and different nature. It is hard to assess the impact of these commentaries and forewords to books published by scholars and friends of Jung. I think, however, that it will not be far wrong to think that Jung himself had a significant effect upon the introduction of eastern religion to a general western audience. Did not Jung's introduction to the *I Ching*, for example, with his theory of synchronicity and his practical example of using the oracle, help in the understanding and popularization of a text which might otherwise have been seen as an abstruse magical book? Jung's theory and impact have certainly aided in western appreciation of eastern religion and thought.

Yet, who would have imagined in the 1930's or even when Jung died in 1961, that eastern religion would descend like an avalanche into the west and gobble up a significant proportion of spiritually hungry youth and adults within a short time? Jung, no doubt, would have been horrified by this wholesale embracing of alien religions and abandonment of western foundations. He keeps saying as much in warnings throughout his various introductions. In his "Yoga and the West," for example, in that same Vol. 11, he

I

acknowledges a great appreciation of the psychological material revealed by yoga, but asserts directly that the *technique* is really bad for us westerners, since we need to *open* up to the unconscious and not to move away from the fantasies, etc. which emerge in meditation. Our western rationalism, he avers again and again, has caused us a cramp of consciousness and we must allow these contents to be embraced by us. (Parenthetically, it is generally known that Jung, himself, employed Yoga exercises when over-whelmed by emotion, in order to calm himself sufficiently, to even begin his confrontation with the unconscious via active imagination).

Eastern spirituality, with its age-old appreciation of introversion and receptivity to the non-material aspect of life, can well do what it does since it sinks into and rises out of its depth, rather like the lotus, whereas many of us - with our endless attempts at mastery for its own sake - will often kill it by an "engineering" attitude or succumb to ill-fitting ideas. Listen to a quote from Jung along these lines:

> I wish particularly to warn against the oft-attempted imitation of Indian practices and sentiments. As a rule nothing comes of it except an artificial stultification of our Western intelligence. Of course, if anyone should succeed in giving up Europe from every point of view, and could actually *be* nothing but a yogi and sit in the lotus position with all the practical and ethical consequences that this entails, evaporating on a gazelle-skin under a dusty banyan tree and ending his days in nameless non-being, then I should have to admit that such a person understood yoga in the Indian manner. But anyone who cannot do this should not behave as if he did. He cannot and should not give up his Western understanding; on the contrary, he should apply it honestly without imitation or sentimentality, to understand as much as is possible for the Western mind (par. 933, Vol. 11).

Jung did not know of the many westerners who, since that time, have done just that - evaporate on gazelle skins. It is quite true that of all the youth who began to uncritically submit to Eastern disciplines, many just "dropped out" of the work, when they discovered how much effort and devotion over a long period was really required. Others, just as Jung observed, emerged as strange creatures wearing Eastern peacock tails and seemed, at best, bizarre or foolish. There have been a significant number of people, on the other hand, who have been able to immerse themselves in Eastern techniques and viewpoints, not only at no cost to their psychic health, but with an expansion of consciousness that would not otherwise be possible.

Jung was not in error, however, when he pointed out that the mere assimilation of a new or foreign viewpoint, thus loosing ones roots, is not an attractive proposition. Better to hold one's own - if we are Westerners - and apply our brand of criticism and attitude to imagination. Yet it is certainly possible to immerse oneself and appreciate our opposite number in order to arrive at a greater wholeness. This volume, indeed, presents the efforts of an Easterner, Dr. Miyuki, and a Westerner, myself, who do try to hold their own and yet integrate the "other". I did Zen meditation, alone and with my friend, Dr. Miyuki, for seven years, with great personal benefit and deepened understanding of the Buddhist experience. I did so without sacrificing Western ways of meditation and prayer. Others have done the same.

Jung's great gift was to discriminate and integrate, a rare commodity in the world, and one for all of us, East and West, to cultivate in ourselves. Let us quote once more from Jung's writing, this time from his commentary for "The Tibetan Book of the Great Liberation," in which he compares East and West:

> We in the West believe that a truth is satisfactory only if it can be verified by external facts. We believe in the most exact observation and exploration of nature; our truth must coincide with the behavior of the external world, otherwise it is merely "subjective." In the same way that the East turns its gaze from the dance of *prakriti* (physis) and from the mutitudinous illusory forms of *maya*, the West shuns the unconscious and its fantasies (Vol. 11, par. 487).

Jung goes on to say that even though the East has an introverted attitude, it can deal with the external world, and that the West deals with the internal world of psyche via the Church. They both have value and insufficiency, but it is a mistake to mix them up. He goes on:

> To jump straight. . .into Eastern yoga is no more advisable than the sudden transformation of Asian peoples into half-baked Europeans. I have serious doubts as to the blessings of Western civilization, and I have similar misgivings as to the adoption of Eastern spirituality by the West.

Then, finally, Jung informs us:

> Yet the two contradictory worlds have met. The East is in full transformation; it is thoroughly and fatally disturbed. Even the most efficient methods of European warfare have been

successfully imitated. The trouble with us seems to be far
more psychological. Our blight is ideologies. . .

Since Jung's day, East and West have met even more fully. Japan
is more efficient than the West at its own game, and it is clear that
Eastern spirituality has invaded the United States and Europe in
an unexpectedly powerful way. The issues that Jung pointed out
are still with us today. After twenty-five years, it may be time to
re-examine those issues once more. That is the background for
this book.

When I was studying in Zurich in the late 1950's, there was only
one representative from the East, a Hindu professor from India
(Arwind Vasavada), who proved to be the first of that region to
become a Jungian Analyst. Since that time, only a few more
Easterners have undergone Jungian training, from Japan primarily,
but also from Korea. It is likely that the number of Asians involved
with Jungian Analysis will increase dramatically and now might be
the time to take stock.

The present book presents the findings, both personal and
impersonal, of two Jungian Analysts who have been propelled, by
fate and psychic trajectory, to take up the encounter with the
"other." How successful we are at that, we leave the reader to
decide. I believe, however, that Jung would be very pleased,
indeed, to have his works so seriously studied by a Japanese
Buddhist priest of many generations inheritance. Dr. Miyuki is
certainly the first Jungian to be fully steeped in both Eastern
Religion and Western tradition, so that his work, gathered from
several places, is especially welcome for those of us similarly
propelled to engage in the East-West encounter. I feel privileged to
be sharing this book with him. Our relationship has been part of
that "ecumenical" process that the collective psyche has been
engaging in for some time. Who of us can forget, after reading
Jung's *Memories, Dreams and Reflections*, his discovery in his dream of
the Yogi, that he was both meditator and meditated upon? The
psyche, at work with him as a forerunner, continues its development
and it is a pleasure for us to offer our own results dedicated to his
spirit.

In Part 1 of this book, Dr. Miyuki and I each write an account of
how East and West have met each other in our own souls. My
contribution is one that I presented in Tokyo in the spring of 1982
at just such an occasion of an East-West symposium. Dr. Miyki's is
written expressly for this volume. I think that the reader will be as
moved as I was upon reading this profound account of East-West
experience in a man who so deeply embodies the Eastern psyche,

yet was literally assaulted into coming to the West and finding a unification of these opposites. In reading it, I was once more reminded of my own dream of him, when I first met him, and long before there was any idea of him becoming a therapist. In it, he had the mark of the fox cult upon his face, which was said to be a sign of a healer. Shortly after I had this dream, I read an article in which the fox cult of ancient Japan was described. In that cult, the fox was connected with the shaman. At that time, Dr. Miyuki had no interest whatsoever in becoming an analyst or healer; he had entered analysis to further understand East and West in himself and to pursue his own development. It was only several years later that this possibility presented itself and he went to Zurich to study.

I am very grateful to have shared this long relationship and to experience, with him, the "sense of boundlessness" together.

Part II is taken up with those marvellous images of the Zen path to Enlightenment, the Ox-herding Pictures. Dr. Miyuki's contribution is from a previously published article. My article was expressly written for this work and is one I am particularly pleased to have had the chance to do. The pictures have been a friend to me for more than a quarter-century and I am grateful for the opportunity to put on paper the reflections and insights I have gleaned from them over the years. The tale of *The Ronin*, which follows, is taken from my fictional story of individuation in ten people, *The Tree*. It represents a Western man's way of honoring that part of his psyche which was Japanese and Buddhist.

Part III includes several of Dr. Miyuki's papers on various aspects of Buddhism and Jungian psychology, in which he convincingly demonstrates the error of the Western assumption that Buddhism requires the "dissolution" of the ego. Rather, he points out, the ego is strengthened in meditation, and what is "dissolved" is ego-centricity. One becomes "Self-centric," as he describes in both story and concept.

Finally, as an "Afterword," I have presented some further thoughts which may bring the matter up to date.

In all, our work can be seen as an offering to, and carrying on of, the very spirit of "Jung" that Dr. Miyuki writes about. It is to the embodied Jung to whom we both owe a thanks which goes beyond our capacity to express adequately.

J. Marvin Spiegelman
Studio City, California
May 1985, The Year of the Ox

Part One

EAST AND WEST FROM THE PERSONAL POINT OF VIEW

EAST AND WEST:
A Personal Statement
By J. Marvin Spiegelman

(Originally presented at the East-West Symposium in Tokyo, Japan, Spring 1982)

What follows is a personal statement: reminiscence, dream, fantasy and fact, interpretation and conjecture, all aimed at expressing my own experience of the conflict and union of East and West, seen from a psychological standpoint. By that I mean, inner image and outer event are fused, sometimes with intent, sometimes not, but the emergent picture, like a personal history, is a construction, a story.

It is from stories that psychological truth emerges, a truth not opposite to science but different. It is different in that the "personal equation" can never be removed; it can only be discriminated by going deeper, plunging into those depths of the subjective where the psyche becomes transpersonal, general, archetypal. So this is my intent: to illuminate the general via the individual.

My first personal experience of the East begins in the spring of 1940 when, as a lad not yet fourteen, I had begun high school. In one of my classes, second year Spanish, there were several Japanese girls, all Nisei, who captured my imagination. They were very different from one another, these girls: Ruby Okubo was enormously bright; Yuki Mishima cute and pert; Kimiko Naruse quite beautiful; Louise Yamazaki warm-hearted and good-natured. But all of them were polite, disciplined, very dedicated to learning and to good work. These girls, along with several capable Jewish

3

students, made that one of the most energetic, productive, and challenging classes that I ever had. Until that time, I had been a rather good student and did not need to work terribly hard in order to get high grades. But these girls memorized every lesson! All the vocabulary, all the grammar, everything! In order to keep up appearances, I had to do something similar. As a consequence, this class soared with good work, much to the delight of Mrs. Snyder, an elderly teacher who was excellent in her skills and attitude.

I always looked forward to this class, and enjoyed the subtle skirmishes with Ruby. In the end, Ruby won, since she took first place in the school Spanish medal, but I was a close second. It was good for me to be second for a change, but even better for me than that was the experience my soul had in taking in the beauty and wonder of those Nisei girls.

One might say, naturally, that I fell in love with them, but our relationship was at a distance. Only a few words could be exchanged, and only the common task, Spanish, be discussed. In those years, there were great barriers between the ethnic groups that comprised Los Angeles. But I felt a close kinship with the girls since I, too, was of a minority which was both admired and despised, the Jewish one, and I, too, was a kind of Nisei, although my mother was only an infant when she was brought to the United States and my father only a young man out of his teens when he arrived. I did not know then that these girls touched and evoked my own feminine nature, my *anima*, in her delicate, sensitive, devoted and passionate nature. I am eternally grateful to them. That their names are still with me, after all these years, is a mark of their impact.

The class that year was not my final experience of them. I am deeply chagrined and pained to have to report what follows. Two years later, in the spring of 1942, I watched with horror as these lovely Japanese girls, along with all the other Japanese boys and girls in our school, were forced to leave the area and were packed off, along with their families, to what were called "re-location centers." It was clear to most of us at the time that these people were no threat whatsoever to the United States or its war effort, but that they were victims of American prejudice and, particularly, California hysteria. I had also known that prejudice, in a less virulent form, in the thirties, toward my own ethnic group. We were kin, therefore, yet apart. When they wept, I wept also, in helpless frustration and sorrow.

Some years ago, I tried to locate them again but could not. It is here, therefore, as I speak to you in the place from which these wonderful girls have their ethnic origin, that I express my deep sadness at their pain and ill-treatment. I acknowledge my shame that my great-hearted and tolerant country could be so narrow-spirited and mean. I also express my regret that I did not speak up more, in protest. All I could do, then, was to say to them that I was sorry that this happened, that I did not feel them to be enemies. I hope that they believed that. But the subsequent capacity to forgive and forget on the part of the American Japanese is known to you and it is in appreciation of that spirit that I feel that I can even speak today about that event. I, a member of a people who has nearly been destroyed by a holocaust, can attest that the darkness of the human soul falls upon us all. If we do not somehow cope with our collective shadows or dark side in a more conscious way, and with less projection, there will be no minorities one day, and perhaps, no people left at all.

It was not a sermon, however, that I planned to deliver here, but to tell the story of my connection between East and West. What can one conclude from this early experience? That a native Californian, born in a land facing the orient could feel the impact of the culture of Japan in his life, and note its effect in his soul. Such impact did exist and, as you will see, had long-range effects.

During the years immediately before and after my encounter with my high school friends, I had other experiences of the Japanese and their culture, such as the shops and restaurants of Little Tokyo in my native city of Los Angeles, and an occasional meeting with a Japanese person, but no other meeting had as much impact upon me as did the girls.

My next profound experience of the East came during World War II, when I was a sailor in the Merchant Marine and travelled around the world. During those travels in war-time, I spent a month in Calcutta, India and two weeks in Columbo, Ceylon, both of which touched me quite profoundly, but differently from the spirit of Japan. I shall not dwell here on their impact, but I want to say that India, in the end, meant Hinduism to me and Japan meant Buddhism, but also something more and other. It is with the particular Japanese form of Eastern psychology of Being that I wish to be concerned with here. For this concern, my next experiences of the East came not from without but from within.

After the war, I resumed my studies and decided to become a psychologist. Ultimately, I knew that I wanted to be a clinical psychologist and a Jungian Analyst, so I began my personal analysis during my graduate school days, in 1950. This experience of my own soul, via dreams and fantasies, was a refreshing flooding of what had been a dry, rationalistic viewpoint. It was not long before the Japanese psyche once again entered my consciousness. During that first winter of analysis, I was working with my fantasies and painting them as well, when I became obsessed with the western Christmas carol that begins, "We three kings from orient are. . ." The music is lovely and haunting, and the words speak of the magi who came to honor the infant Jesus in his barnyard crib. For me, however, the fantasy that emerged was of three kings coming to visit a newly born *image of the divine*, not necessarily Jesus. The three kings were, respectively, a Jewish rabbi, a Christian priest, and a Japanese Buddhist priest. I did not know it then, but this "ecumenical" gathering was to play a continuing and powerful role in my psyche. This ultmately lead to the first fiction that I wrote, many years later, which I called "psycho-mythology." In that book, called *The Tree*, there were several different people, of different religions and races, each seeking his or her individuation.

I completed my doctorate in 1952, worked clinically in both the Veterans Administration and the Army, completed my first analysis and married. From 1956 to 1959, I studied at the C.G. Jung Institute in Zurich, Switzerland, realizing a dream I had cherished every since beginning personal analysis. My wife and I were deeply involved with our European roots, as well as in visiting the place of our ancestral origin in Israel. This did not prevent the East and Japan from entering my psyche in unexpected ways.

Midway in my training analysis in Europe, I was struggling with a dark, negative image of the feminine in my psyche. Dream after dream found me trying to placate or silence a shrill, witch-like figure who would not be stilled nor solaced. In one dream she took the form of a Japanese woman who was bitterly, harshly, and bitingly attacking a Japanese man. Her words were like bullets and he, in turn, fired a machine gun at her which had no deathly effect, but there was obvious hurt and emotional bloodshed on both sides. As the host of this painful and bloody psychic conflict, I followed the method of active imagination, invented by Jung, and "dreamed the dream onward." That is to say, I continued with the event in fantasy, allowing my consciousness to play a role in the story. I placed myself between these two warring parties and asked the woman what she wanted. She said, using American slang, that she wanted to "wear the pants," meaning that she wanted the masculine authority. She was tired of being passive and submissive and would have no more of it. In exhaustion and resignation, I turned to the Japanese male aspect of myself and said, "For God's sake, let her have what she wants and let us put an end to this ceaseless war and bloodshed!" He, mindful of the pain that it was causing me as well as himself, agreed, and lay down his weapon. The woman then said, "The pants, please!" She then proceeded to pull out a pair of work pants from behind a large bookcase filled with all my favorite volumes.

I noted, in the fantasy, that my masculinity seemed to lie in the books, in my high valuation of learning. The woman ignored the books, however, and immediately put on the trousers with great alacrity. As she did so, there was a sudden and amazing change of atmosphere and feeling. Once this bitter and vicious person fulfilled her desire and put on the pants, she was transformed into a sweet, tender, sensitive and delicate woman of great beauty. The pants turned into soft silk and suited her perfectly. She was now carrying a tray filled with delectables and was holding it before her as she bowed with both pride and modesty. At the same moment that the woman was transformed, the man also changed. He became a large, grounded, meditating figure, no longer wearing pants, but wearing a robe which was like a long dress. He was profoundly absorbed in his meditation and then I realized that he was revering the Buddha within himself!

The woman was now happily bowing before and serving this carrier of a divine image! I marvelled at this transformation, of course, and was deeply moved by what I had witnessed. The negative feminine, desiring to be aggressive, became active in serving the highest inner value, an image of the Self. Her "animus-ridden" vitriol was transformed into sweet *eros*. His negative defensiveness and impotent aggression, on the other hand, was transformed into a quiet acceptance. His activity became an inner search. It was a turning point for me, for which I was deeply grateful.

You will not be surprised, therefore, when I tell you that a Japanese theme also presented itself at the very end of my analysis in Switzerland. Among my final dreams, there were two which melded almost into one. Here is the first one:

> I am in the office of my analyst, Dr. Meier. We are intensely occupied with the analytic work which then becomes a kind of wrestling match. We move about the floor, generating both intense heat and also light, which shines around us. The event reminds me of pictures of Japanese Sumo wrestlers, although we are clothed. Finally, the match is over and Dr. Meier bows before me, in a both appreciative and mocking manner. I then warmly shake his hand and bid him goodbye. As I leave his office, I also say goodbye to his secretary who is, actually, the

secretary of the Institute. I walk further down a road and meet
my maternal grandmother who greets me most seriously.
She points, silently and solemnly, to a small brick building.
The one-room structure has no windows but is completely
open at the roof to a beautiful, star-filled, night sky. I can see
into this room, although it is bricked in, and I am aware of a
strong, very passionate man. He is writing furiously, occasionally
stopping as if to speak with an unknown comrade. He also
points to heaven, as if addressing God. End of dream.

It is striking for me that this dream presents and summarizes
the analytic work as a kind of wrestling match, Japanese style.
Surely my analyst carried the image of the Self for me, during the
process, and both the heat of passion and the light of consciousness
were generated in this work. That he both bows and mocks at the
end, indicates that he appreciates my effort but he also subtly
precludes any inflation. This seems a fitting climax to this period
of engagement in the life-long process of the relationship between
ego and Self. I think it is worth noting that the Japanese theme
returns powerfully. This time, however, the battle is a male one,
with no damage, and it is the Self who bows to ego, whereas
before it was the *anima* who bowed to the Self. In this dream, I also
bid adieu to the secretary of the Institute, who was also a helper
and friend, and, thereby, say farewell to my studies and kinship
with the Jungian community in Zurich. I am led, thereafter, by
grandmother, the Great Mother in Jungian language, to view a
strange and intense recluse. He continues a process of struggle,
but in the form of writing, closed off from the world in a most
introverted way. He is open, however, to the *lumen naturae*, the
sparks of light and consciousness in the unconscious itself,
symbolized by the starry heavens, and to God Himself. I could not
know then, of course, but just such a form of writing presented
itself to me more than seven years later, about which I shall say
more presently. Here, however, it is worth noting that this ending
dream was predictive internally.

Let me now relate the second dream, which came hard on the
heels of the first:

I am first officer (chief mate) on a merchant ship which is
leaving central Europe for the United States. I stand on the top
deck with the Captain, who is a "radiating presence" as well as
a person. We are aware that the ship goes over land and sea,
across the Alps to Italy, then through the Mediterannean and
the Atlantic Ocean, down around the Cape in South America
and up the Pacific Ocean to Los Angeles. One important
feature of this ship is that the top deck is circular in form and

rotates slowly on a central axis, so that it makes a full rotation in twenty-four hours.

When the ship arrives at Los Angeles Harbor, it changes into a large truck and goes ashore. A young sailor gets off in Pasadena and we proceed to the beach at Santa Monica. There the Captain and I leave the ship and stand on the shore. To our right, there is a Greek temple in which a red-headed woman has died. It is sad, but the Captain and I nod about the vicissitudes of life. We then look out over the Pacific and see that the sun is rising. It is quite paradoxical: the sun is rising in the West and I think of the Land of the Rising Sun. End of dream.

In this dream, the Self is represented in several ways. It is no longer in the form of my analyst, but now takes an unknown personal form, as the Captain, whom I serve as first officer. This is a development from the previous representations in that the image is more individual, comes closer to my personal consciousness, and shows a more harmonious relationship between ego and Self. But there are some impersonal forms of the Self as well: at first there is the ship, a vessel carrying the entire personality; there is also the circular representation of the top deck, with its sense of movement in time, and in relation to the solar day. This theme of the Self as larger and impersonal is repeated in the final portion of the dream where the Sun now carries this symbol. The Sun rises from the West *contra naturam*, as they say in alchemy, implying individuation at deeper levels. That the source of light was from the Land of the Rising Sun suggested that my consciousness was to benefit from the light of oriental wisdom.

In a number of ways, this dream was not only true in an inner sense, as was the first dream, but it also predicted or anticipated outer events. For example, when I returned to America, I had no money and no possibility of starting a practice. I also had the immediate need of caring for my pregnant wife. I took a job, therefore, like the young sailor of the dream, with an industrial psychology firm in Pasadena. This did not last long, as the dream suggests. I also sufferred many disillusionments in the years afterward, as is suggested by the death of the red-headed *anima* in the Greek temple. That *anima* has had many a death and rebirth for me in our rationalistic culture, but she has always returned with great vitality and love. In our present context, however, I want to tell how that rising Sun became quite literal for me.

In December 1959, the same year that I returned from Zurich, I met Hayao Kawai, who was a Fulbright Fellow at the University of California at Los Angeles. He had come to study with my former teacher, Professor Bruno Klopfer. I, too, was a lecturer in the field in which we were both interested, Projective Techniques and the Rorschach ink-blot test. Kawai, who was then Mr. rather then Dr., expressed interest in Jungian analysis and so came to work with me. We labored intensively for the next fourteen months. Here, indeed, was a concrete representative from the Land of the Rising Sun, a young psychologist who was to become the first Jungian Analyst in Japan! The meeting, therefore, was fated, on an objective level, as my dream suggested.

Kawai returned to Japan after his fellowship ended, earning a doctoral degree and then went to Zurich to attend the C.G. Jung Institute. I met him there in 1963, when I returned for a visit, and spent some very pleasant time with him and his family. My young nephew, who was wandering the world then, came with me to visit Dr. Kawai and his family. He was very moved by the experience and said to me, "It was like spending a day in Japan." As you know, Dr. Kawai returned to Japan to become the main carrier of Jungian thought there, until this day. So this exchange of East and West continued in a fashion larger than the individuals concerned.

Nor did these "exchanges of sun-light," one might say, end there. When Dr. Kawai left Los Angeles in February 1961, he referred another analysand to me, Mokusen Miyuki, with whom I worked in analysis for four years. Whereas Dr. Kawai had been a psychologist like myself, and our connection began through clinical psychological instruments like the Rorschach, Dr. Miyuki was a Buddhist priest, and our connection was more of a psychological/religious one. After completing his work with me, Dr. Miyuki also went to Zurich to study, and analysed with my teacher, Dr. Meier, as did Dr. Kawai. Miyuki, too, completed his studies and returned to Los Angeles to both teach at the University and to practice as a Jungian Analyst. Our connection together resumed and has continued ever since. During his first year back, we met weekly to meditate and chat. The second year, my wife and a colleague joined us. Gradually others joined -- a Roman Catholic Priest and Nun, also former analysands of mine. That meditation group, numbering about eight people, lasted with great value and joy for seven years. We would meditate for an hour, then study a *koan*, led by Dr. Miyuki, and then enjoy wonderful food and wine. Years later, when the food and wine became more important than the meditation and discussion, it was time for that group to end.

More recently, however -- a year ago -- I started what came to be known as a Psycho-Ecumenical group. In this group, there are an orthodox Jewish Rabbi, a Roman Catholic Priest, two Catholic Nuns, an Episcopal Priest, a Protestant Church of Christ Minister, Dr. Miyuki and myself. We are all psychotherapists and my seven colleagues are members of the clergy as well. We have worked together on the problems in being both a clergy-person and a psychotherapist. The group continues this year in sharing the various liturgies and rituals.

One can see that my initial dreams and experiences have bourne fruit, sometimes in a very concrete way. I have, of course, also worked analytically with other Japanese people, as well as with some Nisei. So the exchange continues. And now, here are Dr. Miyuki and myself in the spring of 1982, around the time of Buddha's birthday, visiting and speaking together in Japan along with Dr. Kawai and his associates. It feels to me that our presence here and the correspondence in time of Buddha's birthday, Jewish Passover, and Christian Easter is more than ever a realization of my image, long ago, of the three kings celebrating the birth of the divine child.

What is the meaning of this exchange of consciousness, East and West? Is it, as my dream hinted, that western rationalism, born of the creative Greek thought of Plato, Socrates and Aristotle, and finding a great flowering in science, has finally caused ruin to the passionate and emotional western *anima* (the red-head of my dream), and that some of us now need to look to the Orient for consciousness? I think that is true for many, like myself. In a larger sense, the psyche is trying to incorporate all the religions and ethnicities of the earth in order to create a larger synthesis. This goal, I hope, does not aim at replacing any of them, but towards building a larger temple of the soul where all individuals and groups might find a treasured place. I have seen some dreams which hint at that.

As for my own psyche, it is clear that such a circumambulation has clearly been presaged and sought after. My soul has longed to experience deeply each great aspect of West and East and, from within itself, to taste those aspects of the divine manifesting in many languages, myths and visions. One of the better vehicles for that expression has come in my fictional writing, as I mentioned earlier, and was hinted at in the dream I had when I completed my work in Zurich. That wild-eyed man, in that bricked-in room open to the stars, manifested himself seven years later, when I began writing my "psycho-mythology," as I call it. My first book, *The Tree*, as I have mentioned, contained stories of individuation on the part of ten different representatives of as many races, religions and philosophies.

One of these stories was that of a Japanese Ronin, a man who sought his individuation by means of the path represented in the Zen Ox-herding pictures. I had come upon these pictures some years earlier, in 1960, in that most excellent book by Daisetz Suzuki, *Manual of Zen Buddhism*. When I saw the ten pictures in his book, I was captured, in an introverted way, as I was by the experience of the Nisei girls many years before. That is to say, my soul was touched. Finally, in 1967, around the time of Buddha's birthday, I wrote the story of the Ronin who appeared in my psyche, and it is incorporated in *The Tree*. I was originally going to read to you excerpts from that story, since it presented a statement of an aspect of the East as it expressed itself in my own soul. I decided, however, after fifteen years to look at these pictures anew and see what my soul would say about them now. The result follows, with deep respect to the original pictures and to the description and verses of the great Kaku-an of the fifteenth century.

I   Searching for the Ox

All my life I have been searching for the ox, searching, searching. My own nature eludes me. I find it and lose it, spy it and run from it. Must it be so? Kaku-an says that the creature has "never gone astray," it is only I who continually violate my own inward nature, and it is so, it is so. But why? Why do I find and lose, why never content? Speak to me ox, tell me! But the ox speaks not. I only wait and meditate in the forest of my own emptiness.

II   Seeing the Traces

"All vessels are of gold and the world is a reflection of the Self," says Kaku-an and all the wisdom I have gleaned is as nought when I am not within the gate. All books and all knowledge, even all my past enlightenment, is as saw-dust when I am not in communion with my own nature. Why do I leave the precious precincts, how do I find myself outside the gate? Who can tell me? Is it the ox who leaves? Is it I who leave the ox? None can say.

III   Seeing the Ox

Yes, I have seen the ox, many times, many times. He has shown himself to me, in his darkness and in his light, in his wonder and glory, and in his abasement. He is, indeed, "like the salt in water and the glue in color." He is heard in the song of the nightingale, yet is not the song; heard in the stirrings of desire, yet is not the desire. Yes, I have seen him, not just traces. I have seen him in the smile of my wife, in the laughter of my children. I have seen him in my own compassion, my love and appreciation of others. But I have seen him, too, in my own horror, and especially, in the horror in the world. Yes, I have seen him.

IV   Catching the Ox

The ox is caught, I have him in my hands once more. He is unruly and "longs for the sweet-scented field." And he is, as Kaku-an says, hard to keep under control "because of the pressure of the outside world." Is he not, too, in that outside world? But, I have only myself to blame, for the world will not bend to my will, benevolent or not. Only I can bend, and the "I" will not bend. Ah, vanity, how it "struts up a plateau" only to fall once more into the abyss of despond. And why? Will you speak, oh ox? Will you tell why you wander and flee and are wild?

V   Herding the Ox

"Just herd me, oh man," says the Ox of my soul, "just herd me. Let me not wander; let me not escape into the world of illusion and defilement, let me not wander away." And it is I, oh ox, the vain, petty, distractable "I" that you need. For you are as vain and distractable as I. Together we need to be herded, together we need to be tamed, together we need to be yoked. Neither alone, nor astray, but herded and yoked as one.

But why do you flee, oh ox, when we have been together as one? Why, knowing oneness, do you go astray?

"As you do, my friend," says the ox, "As do you. I go astray and you go astray and there is no answer to the question, 'Why?' "

> "The question itself is a sign of despair
> And a mark of the schism you feel
> An embrace and a sensing and a wordless request
> Brings my soul to you out of the air."

VI   Coming Home on the Ox's Back

Once more we are one, oh ox, once more we are united from two. No chains, no whip, no judgment need sever us now, for we

go along together, sniffing the wind. I hear the paddle of your
paw, you hear the tune on my flute. It is to you that I play, oh ox of
my being, it is to you that I sing my songs. No more need be said.

VII   The Ox Forgotten, Leaving the Man Alone

I sit alone, now, in my eyrie, looking upon the mountain, upon
the moon. No struggle now, only serene, only joyful. Thanks to
you, ox, but you are gone. Only the light, "serene and penetrating,"
is there, and there am I, idly appreciating. The struggle, now a
memory, is a cloud upon the mountain's fastness. And just the
moon speaks. The moon sings songs of stillness, of soft light and
gentle breeze, so exquisite that even tears reduce the stillness.

VIII   The Ox and Man Both Gone out of Sight

"All is empty," says Kaku-an, "the whip, the rope, the man and
the ox. Who can ever survey the vastness of heaven?"
And so it is. The sun was there before the light, the circle before
the man. But what use the light without an eye, what use the
whole without the part?

IX   Returning to the Origin, Back to the Source

And beyond the emptiness, beyond the sun, beyond the light,
there is the source. And what is the source? The Tree, the great
circle in the middle of the space is met by the little circle in the hole
of the tree. Heaven without earth, what is it? For whom is the fish
in the deepest dark sea colored? For whom is the sweet scent of the
tree intended?

X   Entering the City with Bliss-Bestowing Hands

And all things are of Buddha-nature, all things are holy. But
only when they meet and touch, only when they meet. What good
is bliss if not bestowed? What use are hands which do not touch?

A REFLECTION ON MY THIRTIETH YEAR IN THE WEST

By Mokusen Miyuki

Introduction

It has been a little over thirty years since I left Japan. The more I stay in the West, the more "Japanese" I discover myself to be. This may sound peculiar; yet, my awareness of the "Japanese" in me has helped me to be my*self*, the self being shared with others as other *selves*. It is my recent feeling that I am at home with others of different backgrounds while I am my*self* a Japanese. This reminds me of Confucius (551-479 B.C.) saying in the *Analects* that "At thirty my character had been formed."[1] For me, what Confucius refers to as "my character" is my*self* as a meeting ground of East and West, which has been molded for the past thirty years.

I was educated in the traditional Japanese manner when Confucius's teaching was respected. For instance, in middle school, we students bowed with reverence to the *Great Learning (Ta Hsuech)*, one of the Four Sacred Books of Confucianism, before we opened the book. It is, therefore, quite natural for me to have recalled Confucius's saying as I approached my thirtieth year in the West.

This Confucius saying consists of four characters in Chinese, i.e., *san-shih erh-li, san-shih* meaning "thirty" and *erh-li* meaning "then (*erh*) stand (*li*)." These words, therefore, can be translated: "At thirty, I had planted my feet firmly upon the ground."[2] "To stand" means "to become a responsible individual in society." The

15

above mentioned feeling of my*self* as a "Japanese" can be taken as a reflection of "standing firm" as my life in the West reached thirty. It would, then, be significant for me to take advantage of this opportunity and to share my thoughts on some experiences which have made me to be my*self* as I am today.

My articles collected in this book were published during the past several years as my life in the West was approaching thirty. These articles are mostly concerned with a Jungian reading of Buddhist literature in appreciation of his hypothesis of individuation. Jung (1875-1961) also designated individuation as "Self-realization." The German term for Self-realization is *Selbstverwirklichung* which, in my understanding, indicates the innate urge of the Self realizing itself as a paradoxical whole, being the center and circumference of the entire psyche, including both conscious and unconscious. The psychic phenomenon Jung describes as *Selbstverwirklichung* can be viewed as a "Self-centric" condition/function of the psyche, which some of my articles attempt to present.

To tell the truth, I have always been especially interested in his view of individuation as *Selbstverwirklichung* because I have had decisive experiences which can be understood in this way. Without these experiences, my study of Jung and Buddhism might have taken a different direction and focus as well. In the following, therefore, I would like to share some of these experiences which have convinced me of the reality of the phenomenon which Jung maintains as the basic hypothesis of his psychology.

II. A Mandalic Dream of the C.G. Jung Institute, Zurich

It is a great pleasure for me to publish some of my articles related to the theme of Buddhism and Jung's psychology with Dr. J. Marvin Spiegelman, my former analyst, and now colleague and close friend. I strongly feel that the analytical experience I had with him for about four years paved the way for me to make a meaningful encounter of East and West on the psychological level. In my practice as a Jungian analyst, furthermore, I have had the opportunity of having analysands with different backgrounds, i.e., nationality, culture, or religion. So it is with my teaching at California State University, Northridge: in my courses, "An Introduction to Religious Studes," "Buddhism, " or "Religion and Personality," I have had students from all over the world. Since I employ the method which C.G. Jung calls "phenomenological" in my teaching and research, I feel my first analytical experience with Marvin was quite decisive in having made me as I am today. This feeling, I believe, is well expressed in the dream of the C.G.

Jung Institute, which I had toward the close of my first analysis and a few months before I left Los Angeles for Zurich in 1964.

In the dream, the C.G. Jung Institute, was a large square building of four stories with the fourth floor as a train station consisting of a loop line connected with the entire world. Many trains were coming and going from all the countries on earth[3].I woke up with a feeling of wonder. At that time, I very much wanted to go to Zurich to study at the C.G. Jung Institute. This desire, however, was unrealistic in view of my economic situation. Yet, I felt it quite urgent to do so, as if it had been my *karma*, or *ming*, the "mandate" to go to study. Had it been impossible to do so, I honestly felt that it would have been better not to have been born in this particular life.

This irresistible force from within, I think, can be best regarded as an innate urge of the Self to realize it*Self*. This takes place "relentlessly" regardless of the conscious will or external situation. When I had this dream, as I recall clearly, Marvin gave me his wholehearted encouragement to go to Zurich to finish my studies there. These days, in my professional activity as analyst, professor, or priest, I have been living this dream out in meeting various people from all over the world in my capacity as a "Jungian." In this sense, this dream has been "prognostic" and foretold my commitment to the "Jungian" center, through which I have been inseperably connected both spiritually and academically.

This dream of the Jung Institute is mandalic, containing the circle of the loop-line which covers the whole world, the square of the Institute building, and the quarternity indicated by the four stories. Jung regards the mandala as the symbol of the Self, the paradoxical unity being simultaneously the center, the goal, and the totality of the entire psyche. The psychic process represented by mandalic images, accordingly, is that of centering so as to create a new orientation. As a matter of fact, this mandalic dream of mine has provided me with the pattern into which my life has evolved, it has "revolved" around a "Jungian" center within. As such, it has been psychologically "real" in its effects, having made my life open to the inmost core of the "Jungian" community. This psychic phenomenon of the centering act of the entire psyche, I believe, Jung designated as *Selbstverwirklichung*, or "Self-realization," which I have described as the "Self-centric" condition/function of the psyche.[5]

Needless to say, my meeting with the West is still going on. It is widely open to future possibilites so that the total outcome, or meaning, of my mandalic dream still remains unknown. Nevertheless, in thinking of this dream while reflecting on my life, I cannot help but realize a sense of "finality" in reference to the concepts of *karma* and *ming* as well.

The idea of *ming*, which can be translated as "destiny," "fate," "life," or "mandate" in English, has been essential to the Chinese way of life. For instance, Confucius speaks of his realization of *ming* which he felt bestowed upon him by "heaven" (t'ien): "At fifty I knew the Mandate of Heaven (*T'ien-ming*)."[6] To receive "the Mandate of Heaven" means to become *t'ien-tzu*, the son of Heaven or the emperor who governs people according to the will of Heaven. Confucius, at age fifty, must have internalized the Mandate of Heaven as his inner dictate. In my dream of the Jung Institute, this inner dictate is symbolized by the mandalic center of the "Jungian" community, which has given me a sense of finality ever since. To quote Jung, "One could not go beyond the center. The center is the goal, and everything is directed toward that center."[7]

As the concept of *ming* has been the basic premise to Confucianistic culture in the Far East, so is that of *karma* to Buddhist Asia. *Karma*, like *ming*, asks us to understand one's own life as exemplified by the saying of Confucius quoted above. This means that in order to understand the idea of *karma* properly, we are in need of "ontological" imagination -- imagination which enables us to envision the total being of man in the universe. In my view, the term *karma* indicates a process of life, morally neutral, consisting of a dynamic nexus of action/reaction in the entire universe, in contrast to the general understanding of *karma* as a law of moral retribution, which, I think, is based on the monotheistic premise of the Judaeo-Christian West.[8] Hence, the realization of one's own *karma*, like that of one's own *ming* or "mandate," brings with it a sense of finality.

It is noteworthy here that Jung links the concept of archetype with *karma*, which he considers as "a sort of psychic heredity based on the hypothesis of reincarnation."[9] What he means by "psychic heredity" is "the universal disposition" of the psyche into forms or categories of the imagination, analogous to Plato's forms (*eidola*). Being categories of the imagination, these forms are "always in essence visual" and "always and everywhere present."[10] Jung states:

> As the products of imagination are always in essence visual, their forms must, from the outset, have the character of images and moreover of *typical* images, which is why, following St. Augustine, I call them 'archetypes.' Comparative religion and mythology are rich mines of archetypes, and so is the psychology of dreams and psychoses."[11]

It seems that, if *karma* can be taken as an archetype in the sense of "the universal disposition" of the psyche, *ming* as the "predestined" pattern into which psychic life develops can also be understood as an archetype. In thinking of the mandalic dream of the Jung Institute, I often find myself appreciating my life "mysteriously" connected with something beyond, be it karmic nexus, pattern of life, or an archetype. This profound depth of life thus felt, I believe, has been termed in Buddhism as *dharma*, or teaching, of interdependent origination (pratitya-samutpada).[12]

Whatever terms are used to designate my experience of the mandalic dream, the "core" of the phenomenon remains unknown. Herein comes my awareness of the importance of the kind of methodology we employ in dealing with materials from the unconscious, such as dreams, religious experience, or the like, which cannot be fully formulated conceptually or communicated intellectually. As Jung points out, "when something is little known, or ambiguous, it can be envisaged from different angles, and then a multiplicity of names is needed to express its peculiar nature."[13] Jung thus proposes the method of amplification, of which he states: "Amplification is always appropriate when dealing with some dark experience which is so vaguely adumbrated that it must be enlarged and expanded by being set in a psychological context in order to be understood at all."[14]

Following Jung, then, I can regard these words, *karma, ming,* or interdependent origination, as synonymous and amplificatory to one another in pointing to something little known. Nevertheless, taken together, they communicate, without fail, the centering function of the psyche, which can be described as "Self-centric," as attested to by Confucious's conviction of the Mandate of Heaven, at the age fifty, as well as my mandalic dream of the C.G. Jung Institute, Zurich.

III. Three Earlier Experiences

The awareness of the inner center, which is seen in my mandalic dream, has its root in three of my earlier experiences. Like the mandalic dream, I feel these experiences are the expression of the mysterious operation of numerous incomprehensible factors or conditions in my life, which can be considered as the function of *ming* and *karma* as well. They speak for the phenomenon duly called the "Self-centric" functioning of the psyche and, as such, enable me to visualize my *karmic* life as being beyond this life and being related to the cosmic background. Without these experiences, I might not have been interested in studying Buddhism and, consequently, Jung's psychology. To put it another way, these experiences drove me to practice Buddhism and, then, to undergo analysis, as if they had been "caused" by the mandate of the innermost core of my being. These experiences happened to me quite unexpectedly during the Second World War. In this sense, my encounter with the West begins in a dramatic way.

All three experiences took place in 1945, the last year of the Second World War, which ended in August. The first event was in March when my home temple was completely destroyed by the first U.S. incendiary bombing on Osaka, my home city. The second took place on the day when the war was over, and the third on the day just after the war.

The First Experience: I still remember that day well. It was March 14, 1945. Having been commandeered, I went to a war plant in Hirakata city, about fifteen miles to the northeast of Osaka, to make ammunition in the evening. Around midnight, there sounded an air raid alarm. The entire factory stopped working and we sheltered ourselves in the dug-out until dawning. We were informed that Osaka was undergoing an air raid, yet none of us had even the slightest idea that our homes might have been destroyed by the attack. We really enjoyed the whole night's rest. As usual, we were released from night duty at five A.M. and went back to Osaka by a suburban electric railway.

The interurban arrived at the terminal wherefrom my home temple was only a ten minute walk. While walking, I found many houses standing on both sides of the street. Naturally, I expected my home to be safe. When I turned the corner to my home, however, I found no house standing there. The whole area was totally ruined by the last night's attack. I stood silently on the place where my home temple's gate was. It was a moment of stillness, in which the inner and outer worlds merge into one. All of a sudden, I realized that something powerful got "awakened" in me -- an inner spring rushing upward, I felt, from the bottom of my being. I also experienced this, paradoxically, as the sun shining in the clear sky of an early spring morning. The strong sensation of transparency and rootedness in the cosmic center took place, which was followed by a momentary thought, like a flash, that I am both nothing and everything and I am here. I heard, then, someone from behind me informing me that my parents were both safe and waiting for me at the nearby school ground. My parents were given to me anew, I felt, as a precious treasure, just as my life was. With the feeling of serenity and gratitude, I left the ruin for the school ground to meet my parents.

The Second Experience: On August eighth, the U.S. Air Force dropped an atomic bomb on Hiroshima. I remember still vividly that I read in a newspaper that a new kind of bomb, incredibly powerful, was used by the enemy and that, therefore, we all had to be ready to die for our country and emperor. Then, on the fourteenth of August, we were told to listen to the radio carefully because the emperor had something serious to say to us. It was a grave matter for Japanese, at that time, to hear the "flesh voice" of the "living god" of the emperor. My parents and all others, as far as I knew, bowed their heads down while the emperor was addressing us through the radio, although we were not able to hear clearly what he said. Nevertheless, my parents and I felt immediately after this address that the war was over and that Japan had lost the war.

My parents were crying. I, however, was not able to shed a tear; instead, I felt a moment of stillness. Soon, I found myself asking, "Why can't you cry for Japan losing the war? Don't you love your country? Aren't you a Japanese?" These questions, related to my national identity, got narrowed down themselves by the "awakening" I experienced at the ruin of my temple, burnt down by the air attack in March -- the awakening of myself being both nothing and everything in the transparent universe.

The Third Experience: It was a beautiful summer day just after the war. I was so happy because the war was over. I went out to the fields and picked up well-ripened tomatoes to enjoy the fresh taste. Then, I heard an airplane coming toward me. I looked up to find an American plane. I waved both hands to the plane to express my joy -- the war is over, it's so beautiful, and here am I. I assumed, naively, that the pilot on the plane must have been feeling the same as I did. To my great surprise, the plane started to shoot at me. My whole body got stiff and I was petrified there without being able to move an inch. Many bullets hit the ground and formed a line while raising a cloud of dust around me. I realized that it was neither a joke nor a mistake, and I fell down to the ground like a balloon getting deflated. My mind was totally blank. The fear of facing death was missing. Nor was there anger against the pilot. A few seconds later, however, I experienced an indescribable intense hunger for life upsurging from within me. I thought I might go crazy. After a short while, I found myself mystified by the line — like a thread or a thin paper — between life and death. I was convinced that I would not die a meaningless death: there is life (*ming*), there is meaning as destiny (*ming*).

As I recall these experiences, I cannot help but appreciate the operation of *ming*, or that of *karmic* reality, which can be described as the "Self-centric" functioning of the psyche. It is observed in my feeling of "transparency," being simultaneously within and without, in my thought that I am both nothing and everything, in the mystery of the thread or the thin paper between life and death. As in the image of the "Jungian" center being extended to every corner of the world. They all remind me of Jung's view of the Self, or the paradoxical whole, being "Not only the center but also the whole circumference which embraces both conscious and unconscious."[15] The Self being the union of opposites, the "Self-centric" function of the psyche is experienced by an individual as "the paradoxical state/process of simultaneous occurence of emptying/fulfilling, or negating/affirming," which I discussed in the article, "Self-realization in the Ten Oxherding Pictures."[16]

IV. More Reflections

As time goes by, the fortieth year, fiftieth year and so on might come to me as I stay in the West. The pattern and direction provided within the mandalic dream of the Jung Institute, Zurich, would keep developing to enrich and deepen the "Jungian" center within. The image of the Jungian center in the dream is the paradoxical whole, being both the core and the entire world. It also conveys a sense of the continual creation of a "new" center, while getting in touch with the world through the incesssantly incoming "trains." This, symbolically, refers to new psychic situations arising in the world. As Jung says, "No words express the whole and we can grasp only its partial aspect in an inadequate way."[16] In this vein, I am tempted to quote again from the *Analects* as Confucius continues his reflections:

> At fifteen my mind was set on learning. At thirty my character had been formed. At forty I had no more perplexity. At fifty I knew the Mandate of Heaven (*T'ien-ming*). At sixty I was at ease with whatever I heard. At seventy I could follow my heart's desire without transgressing moral principles.[17]

This reflection of Confucius on his life's path appears to coincide with what Jung designates as "the stages of life." In the first half of life, according to Jung, man is expected to establish himself in society. For this sake, he has to go to school, find a job, marry and raise a family. This image of man in the first stage of life is spoken by Confucius as "before he became forty". As man grows older, however, he is more and more destined to experience what can be called the human condition, such as illness, separation, or death, which the Buddha designated as *duhkha*, or *dis-ease*.[18] The experience of this *dis-ease* inevitably makes man aware of the limitation of life.

Facing his finiteness, man begins to think of the meaning of life. This is the second half of life, in which man concerns himself with the adapation to his inner need, in contrast to the first half of life which is centered around adaptation to the external world. Jung regards this second stage of life as beginning at around thirty-five. The image of Confucius who "knew the Mandate of Heaven" at fifty presents the image of a man who suceeded in finding his life's meaning connected with something eternal, "the Mandate of Heaven," having stood firm on life's ground.

Interestingly enough, according to Hinduism, the ideal life consists of four *asramas*, or stages: *brahmacarva*, the period of discipline and education, *garhasthya*, the life of the householder and active worker, *vanaprasthya*, retreat for the loosening of bonds and finally *sannyasa*, the life of the hermit.[19] It goes without saying that the first two *asramas* coincide with Jung's first half of life and the second two *asramas* with Jung's second half of life. Regarding the third *asrama*, or *vanaprasthya*, which literally means "forest dweller," *The Laws of Manu*, a sacred book of Hindu life, states: "When a householder sees his (skin) wrinkled, and (his hair) white, and the sons of his sons, then he may resort to the forest."[20] To enter the period of the forest dweller is to seek the meaning of life. His time and energy is now released from this life. His life is meant to seek something infinite which enables him to transcend life and death, or the *samaric* existence, which is exemplified as the stage of *sannyasa*, the life of the hermit. A *sannyasin*, who belongs to the *sannyasa* period, is an ideal sage-hermit who is liberated from any bondage and attachment. This image of *sannyasin* overlaps with that of Confucius, saying "At seventy I could follow my heart's desire without transgressing moral principles." The difference between Confucius and a *sannyasin*, however, is that the latter is out of the world as a hermit whereas the former is in the world. And yet, this distinction cannot be decisive once we recognize that, for both, being in the world doesn't necessarily contradict being out of the world, provided that they share the virtue of having a link with the infinite. When this is the case, they both can be regarded as living embodiments of the supreme value in their respective cultures.

The foregoing reminds me of one of my favorite thoughts of Jung:

> The decisive question for man is: Is he related to something infinite or not? That is the telling question of his life... In the final analysis, we count for something only because of the essential we embody, and if we do not embody that, life is wasted. In our relationships to other men, too, the crucial question is whether an element of boundlessness is expressed in the relationship.[21]

Jung's view of life emphasizing "the crucial question" in this quotation, in my understanding, is amplificatory to the image of Confucius after age fifty, as well as to that of the second two *asramas* of the Hindu ideal life. They all help me to comprehend what is meant by a "Jungian" as indicated in the mandalic dream of the C.G. Jung Institute, Zurich, which I had some twenty years ago. That is, to be a "Jungian" is, paradoxically, to be "related to something infinite." This means, in turn, to go beyond the boundary that we make as a "Jungian."

Reflecting on my thirty-one years of life in the West, I have tried to articulate some experiences which I consider essential, be it professional or private. This attempt has renewed my sincere appreciation for Marvin who has helped me in making my life meaningful. For the past twenty-three years, since I came to know him, I have always felt my relationship with him as embodying "an element of boundlessness," be it as therapy, group discussions, or our psycho-ecumenical gatherings. In these activities, as well as in our friendship itself, I believe we have shared our spirit of a "Jungian," or a seeker after something infinite and essential. This, in turn, provides a meaningful continuation of my mandalic dream.

REFERENCES

1. Wing-tsit Chan, translated and compiled, *A Source Book in Chinese Philosophy*, (Princeton, N.J.: Princeton University Press, 1963), p. 22.

2. *The Analects of Confucius*, translated and annotated by Arthur Waley (New York: Vintage Books, 1938), p. 88.

3. See my article "A Jungian Approach to the Pure Land Practice of *Nien-fo*," p. 265.

4. See my article "Self-realization in the *Ten Oxherding Pictures*," p. 38.

5. See my article "The Ideational Content of the Buddha's Enlightenment as *Selbstverwirklichung*," p. 101.

6. Wing-tsit Chan, *A Source Book*, p. 22.

7. C.G. Jung, *Memories, Dreams, Reflections*, recorded and edited by Aniela Jaffe: trans. Richard and Clara Winston (New York: Pantheon Books, 1961), pp. 198-199.

8. See my article "The Psychodynamics of Buddhist Meditation, A Jungian Perspective," p. 166.

9. C.G. Jung, "On 'The Tibetan Book of the Dead,' " *Psychology and Religion: West and East. CW* 11, par. 845.

10. *Ibid.*

11. *Ibid.*

12. For the detailed analysis of the term *pratitva-samutpada*, see my article "The Ideational Content," p. 106, note 4.

13. C.G. Jung, *Mysterium Coniunctionis. CW* 14, par. 458.

14. C.G. Jung, *Psychology and Alchemy. CW* 12, par. 403.

15. *Ibid.*, par. 44.

16. C.G. Jung, *Memories, Dreams, Reflections*, p. 354.

17. Wing-tsit Chan, *A Source Book*, p. 22.

18. See my article "Living with *Duhkha*."

19. K.M. Sen, *Hinduism.* (Baltimore, Maryland: Penguin Books, 1961), p. 22.

20. S. Radhakrishnan and C. Moore, *A Sourcebook in Indian Philosophy*, p. 181.

21. C.G. Jung, *Memories, Dreams, Reflections*, p. 325.

Part Two

THE OXHERDING PICTURES OF ZEN BUDDHISM

SELF—REALIZATION
IN THE TEN
OXHERDING PICTURES

By Mokusen Miyuki

In my paper entitled, "A Jungian Approach to the Pure Land Practice of *Nien-fo*." I challenged the prevailing psychological view of Eastern religions as aiming at the "dissolution," or at the least the "depotentiation," of the ego.[1] I argued that the Pure Land Buddhist practice of *nien-fo* (the mental and/or verbal recitation of Amitabha's name), for example, aids the individual to strengthen, rather than dissolve, the ego through the integration of unconscious contents. In this paper, I would like to further support this point by examining the Zen tradition's *Oxherding Pictures*.[2] These pictures are products of the Zen "mind" and express in an art form the experience of *satori* or Zen enlightenment. Since enlightenment is a psychological reality *par excellence*, these pictures can be analyzed by employing Jungian methodology and his conceptual framework, and by viewing them as portraying what C.G. Jung calls "the individuation process."

Although only a few sets of the *Oxherding Pictures* exist today, in the past there must have been several sets of pictures — and those of various numbers. The variety of sets can be inferred from the fact that there are records of differing "verses" which accompany such pictures.[3] The Zen scholar D.T. Suzuki has made two sets of the *Ten Oxherding Pictures* which are well known in the West: namely, the set whose accompanying ten *Prefaces* and *Verses* were written by the twelfth century Zen master Kuo-an (Kaku-an in Japanese) and another earlier version to which the Zen master Pu-ming wrote the ten accompanying *Verses*.[4] The version by Kuo-an has enjoyed wide acceptance in Japan while the one by Pu-ming was popular in China.[5]

Pu-ming's *Ten Oxherding Pictures* portray a wild, black ox that becomes increasingly white as the pictures proceed. These pictures are entitled: (1) Undisciplined, (2) Discipline Begun, (3) In Harness, (4) Faced Round, (5) Tamed, (6) Unimpeded, (7) *Laissez Faire*, (8) All forgotten, (9) The Solitary Moon, and (10) Both Vanished. Evidently, the emphasis in these pictures is placed upon the gradual achievement of *satori* (Zen enlightenment), which is shown by the progressive whitening of the black ox. The concept of whitening that which is black is based on the Buddhist doctrine of *tathagatagarbha*, the realization of the Buddha-nature, or the genuine self, which is obscured by the dark side of the personality.

According to Ts'u-yuan, who wrote the *Preface* to Kuo-an's version, Kuo-an was not satisfied with the idea of a gradual whitening of the ox, nor with the gradual, progressive liberation of the Buddha-nature; thus, he presented his experience of *satori* in a different manner. His pictures are entitled: (1) Searching for the Ox, (2) Seeing the Traces, (3) Seeing the Ox, (4) Catching the Ox, (5) Herding the Ox, (6) Coming Home on the Ox's Back, (7) The Ox Forgotten, (8) The Ox and the Man Both Forgotten, (9) Returning to the Origin, Back to the Source, and (10) Entering the City with Bliss-bestowing Hands. The notion expressed in these pictures is the sudden gain or loss of one's genuine self, as symbolized by the ox.[6]

The Oxherding Pictures have also been referred to as the *Mind-ox Pictures*, thus indicating that the ox, or the genuine self, in the picture represents the Zen concept of "mind."[7] In Chinese Buddhism, the term "*hsin*," "mind," which also refers to the "heart" or essence, has been used interchangeably with the term "*hsing*," which means nature or essence. Accordingly, in Zen the psychic reality connected with the word "mind" is that of *satori* in the sense of "seeing one's own nature" (*chien-hsing*). A famous Zen tenet illustrates this connection:

> **A special transmission outside the scriptures,**
> **Not depending upon letters,**
> **Pointing directly to the Mind (literally "human mind")**
> **See into Nature itself and attain Buddhahood.**[8]

In this tenet the words "mind," "nature," and "Buddhahood" are all used to express different aspects of one and the same reality; namely, *satori*.

The view of *satori* implied in the pictures of both Pu-ming and Kuo-an is to be understood in terms of the doctrine of *tathagatagarbha*, or realization of the Buddha-nature. This doctrine assures the possibility of universal enlightenment and has become basic to the so-called "sinified Buddhism," such as Hua-yen, T'ien-tai, Ch'an (Zen in Japanese), or Ch'ing-t'u (Pure Land). For instance, Chih-yen (602-668 A.D.), the third patriarch of Hua-yen Buddhism, viewed the Buddha-nature as having a tripartite character: (1) the Buddha-nature itself, the genuine essence which is universally ever-present in all beings, although it is in a state of dark ignorance and passion, obscured and defiled; (2) the Buddha-nature as the driving force, (*yin-chu*) or the fundamental urge to realize itself through the practice of *prajna* (wisdom) and *samadhi* (concentration); and (3) the Buddha-nature as perfectly realized through practice.[9] In Zen, as mentioned above, both terms, "mind" and "nature" are used interchangeably in designating the Buddha-nature. Hence, the Zen concept of "mind" refers to something quite different from the Western concept of the word.

Jung was well aware of the fact that the Eastern concept of "mind" is radically different from that in the West. He states; "In the West, 'mind' is more or less equated with consciousness, whereas in the East the word 'mind' is closer to what the West refers to as the unconscious."[10] Jung seems to imply here that in the East the word "mind" designates what he means by the "psyche," or the psychological process which includes both conscious and unconscious. Were this so, the Zen concept of mind could be taken as equivalent to Jung's concept of the total psyche, or the Self.

Jung explains the relationship of consciousness to the unconscious as follows:

> Consciousness, no matter how extensive it may be, must always remain the smaller circle within the greater circle of the unconscious, an island surrounded by the sea; and like the sea itself, the unconscious yields an endless and self-replenishing abundance of living creatures, a wealth beyond our fathoming.[11]

From this viewpoint, then, the *Oxherding Pictures* can be understood as depicting the attempt of the oxherd, or the ego, to creatively relate itself to the inexhaustible treasure of the "mind-ox," or the unconscious. In Kuo-an's version, however, this confrontation of the ego with the unconscious ceases with the seventh picture wherein an "individuated man" is portrayed. Accordingly, the last three pictures by Kuo-an can be taken as describing the life of the genuine man, or the individuated ego, working in the service of the Self in and through common, daily activities.

In writing about individuation, Jung states: "Individuation means becoming a single, homogeneous being, and, in so far as 'individuality' embraces our innermost, last, and incomparable uniqueness, it also implies becoming one's own self. We could therefore translate individuation as 'coming to selfhood' or 'Self-realization.' "[12] The German term *Selbstverwirklichung*, which is translated here as "self-realization" in English, indicates the psychological urge of the Self to realize itself — the Self being the center and the whole circumference embracing both conscious and unconscious psyche. This point is clarified by Edward F. Edinger when he states: "Individuation seems to be the innate urge of life to realize itself consciously. The transpersonal life energy in the process of self-unfolding uses human consciousness, a product of itself, as an instrument for its own self realization."[13]

According to Jung, therefore, individuation begins with the innate urge of the Self for realization, regardless of the conscious will or external situation. To become "a single, homogenous being" is not something the ego can create at will. Being driven by the Self's urge, it becomes possible for the ego, the center of the conscious personality, to evolve. Jung states:

> "The ego stands to the self as the moved to the mover, or as object to subject, because the determining factors which radiate out from the self surround the ego on all sides and are therefore supraordinate to it. The self, like the unconscious, is an *a priori* existent out of which the ego evolves. It is, so to speak, an unconscious prefiguation of the ego. It is not I who create myself, rather I happen to myself."[14]

This fundamental urge of self realization is basic to the creative life of the individual as well exemplified in Jung's *Memories, Dreams, Reflections* which begins with the following statement:

> "My life is a story of the self-realization of the unconscious. Everything in the unconscious seeks outward manifestation, and the personality too desires to evolve out of its unconscious condition and to experience itself as a whole."[15]

The innate urge for self-realization has been designated in Buddhism as that aspect of the Buddha-nature which, to use Chih-yen's conception, is manifested as the driving force to realize itself. The Buddha-nature is always present as Kuo-an states in his *Preface* to the first picture: "The beast has never gone away, and what is the use of searching for him" (p. 129). In Kuo-an's version, the eternal presence of the Buddha-nature as the Self's urge to realize itself is symbolized by the circle in which each of the ten pictures are depicted. For, the circle, which conveys the idea of the non-beginning and non-ending quality of eternity, represents the ever-presence of the Buddha-nature in which Zen practice takes place.

Once the innate urge of the Self to realize itself is activated, the Self relentlessly imposes on the ego the task of integrating the dark side of the psyche, or the unconscious. For as "the smaller circle within the greater circle of the unconscious,"[16] the ego is constantly conditioned by the Self as the determining factor for its existence and development. Since the Self is the paradoxical totality in which the opposites such as conscious and unconscious, light and darkness, good and evil, are united, there is no conscious realization of totality without integration of the opposites. Jung states: "Whenever the archetype of the self predominates, the inevitable psychological consequence is a state of conflict . . . and man must suffer from the opposite of his intention for the sake of completeness."[17] The ego, thus endangered by the demand of the Self's urge to realize itself, is depicted in Pu-ming's version of the *Oxherding Pictures* by the gradual process of whitening, that is, the depotentiating and integrating the wild black ox as the symbol of the overwhelming energy of the unconscious.

Self-realization, or the ego's encounter of the archetype of the Self, is not a neutral experience. As a numinous experience, it exercises a powerful influence on the shaping or reshaping of conscious contents. Jung states:

> . . .the archetypes have, when they appear, a distinctly numinous character which can only be described as "spiritual," if "magical" is too strong a word. Consequently this phenomenon is of the utmost significance for the psychology of religion. In its effects it is anything but unambiguous. It can be healing or destructive, but never indifferent, provided of course that it has attained a certain degree of clarity.[18]

Edward F. Edinger characterized the development of the ego in its confrontation with the Self as a circular process of alternating ego-Self separation and ego-Self union. He states: "Indeed, this cyclic (or better, spiral) formula seems to express the basic process of psychological development from birth to death."[19] In this manner, the progressive differentiation of the conscious life takes place continually throughout life as the result of conscious assimilation of the unconscious contents, or the enrichment of consciousness by the integration of the unconscious. The idea of the progressive enrichment of the conscious life is evidently depicted by Pu-ming, as mentioned above, by the gradual process of whitening, or integrating, the wild black ox, or the unconscious. It is also indicated by Kuo-an in the tenth picture of his version of the *Oxherding Pictures*. In this picture "Entering the City with Bliss-bestowing Hands," the scene of an old man meeting a young boy in the market place is portrayed, showing thus that enrichment of conscious life in and through common activities, such as meeting or greeting people on the street. With this last picture, the development of the ego reverts to ordinary life depicted in the first picture but on a richer level of consciousness.

Psychologically speaking, the circle symbolizes the *temenos*, the magic circle, or the protective function of the Self. The ego consciousness, as mentioned above, constantly faces the danger of being assimilated by the menacing energy of the unconscious. If it is to resist assimilation and be protected from the danger of fragmentation or disintegration, it is of prime importance for the ego to be strengthened by integrating the unconscious contents. In self-realization, the Self, which is the paradoxical totality, provides the ego with the strength and stability for its development while it simultaneously imposes on the ego the task of integrating the dark side of the personality. The protective function of the Self is indicated, in Kuo-an's version of the *Oxherding Pictures*, by the circle in which each of the ten pictures are depicted, representing thus the ever-presence of the Buddha-nature, or the Self, which provides the practitioner with strength and stability. The square in which Pu-ming portrayed each of the ten pictures in his version can also be taken as showing the utmost importance of the integration of the unconscious into consciouness, being supported by the Self's protective function.

In Zen practice, the archetype of the Self is projected onto the master as the ideal self-image; hence, the encounter of the ego with the Self takes place, as projected on the master-disciple relationship. Accordingly, Zen emphasizes the importance of meeting the "right" master for the disciple in seeking for a genuine realization of *satori*. The encouragement as well as the admonition of the master provides the disciple with the *temenos* within which the latter's psychological security is gained. Being thus protected from an unconscious outburst and disintegration, the disciple can attempt to creatively relate himself to the treasure house of the Buddha-nature or the unconscious.

Jung has observed that in the numinous experience, or the confrontation with the Self, mandala symbolism often emerges in the manifested unconscious materials, such as dreams, fantasies, psychic episodes, myths, fairytales, and such religious depictions as the *Oxherding Pictures*.

According to Jung, a mandala is a symmetrical structure consisting of ternary or quaternary combinations which are concentrically arranged. The ternary combinations symbolize the dynamic process of development or growth, whereas the quaternay configurations represent a static structual wholeness, or completion.[20] Jung's observation about the combination of the numbers three and four can be seen in the first seven pictures in Kuo-an's *Ten Oxherding Pictures*. Were it possible for us to understand the third picture, "Seeing the Ox," as representing the Zen "goal" of "seeing into Nature itself,"[21] then, the fourth picture, "Catching the Ox," can be taken as representing attained wholeness or completion. Since self-realization is cyclic or spiral, as symbolized by the empty circle, the achieved totality is both the end and the beginning. Thus, as soon as the fourth state is realized, a new struggle begins on a higher level of consciousness. The new process thus initiated in the fourth picture reaches its culmination in the sixth picture, with the seventh picture, as the fourth of this second series, depicting the completion of the second ternary process. Therefore, in the first seven pictures, we can observe two sets of processes: the process from the first to the third picture with the fourth as the completion, and the process from the fourth to the sixth picture with the seventh as a second completion. Since the number seven comprises the union and totality of the ternary process and the quaternary completion, the seventh picture can be taken as portraying a final accomplishment.

The view that the seventh picture of Kuo-an's version is symbolic of the completion of the process is supported by the title, "The Ox Forgotten, Leaving the Man Alone." In the preceding pictures, individuation or self-realization — in terms of the dialectical confrontation of the ego (the oxherd) and the Self (the ox) — has led the individual to experience a transformation of personality symbolized as "the Man." Kuo-an states in his *Verse*: "Where Lo! the ox is no more [in Sanskrit, literally "emptied"]; the man alone sits serenely" (p. 132). Thus, the ox, the Self, has "emptied" itself to become the "man." With this seventh picture, the oxherding scenes cease and the "man" is depicted instead of the ox. In Pu-ming's version, this individuated man is portrayed in the ninth picture, entitled "The Solitary Moon."

In Kuo-an's *Ten Oxherding Pictures*, therefore, *satori* as the on-going process is depicted as three sets of processes; namely, the initial process from the first to the third picture with the fourth as the completion; the continuing process from the fourth to the sixth picture with the seventh as a second completion, which is followed by the life of the "individuated ego," or the "Self-centered ego," the ego which functions in the service of the Self, portrayed from the eighth to the tenth pictures. This third process reverts to the first picture as a third completion, returning thus to the "beginning" on a different level of consciousness.

The genuine "man" in the seventh stage must face, and struggle with another serious problem, or *duhkha* ("dis-ease"), precisely because this is the final state of achievement for the ego that has attempted conscious assimilation of unconscious contents. At this stage, individuation as the confrontation of the ego with the Self ceases as such; for, as far as the ego is concerned, there are no resources to draw upon in order to affect any change regarding the realization of the next stage. This stage can manifest as the perilous state of psychic stagnation against which it is said that the ego has no means to cope. This danger of psychic stagnation has been recognized in Buddhism and designated as "the danger of the Bodhisattva, or [of] the seeker for the ultimate enlightenment sinking into *sunyata*, or "emptiness."

According to the *Dasabhumi-sutra*, the *Sutra* of the Ten 'Stages,'" which describes the ten stages of the Bodhisattva's spiritual progress, the Bodhissattva faces the danger of "sinking into *sunyata*," especially when he arrives at the seventh stage called the "Far-going" which follows the realization of the truth of "Inter-dependent Origination" at the sixth stage.[22] Since no means is available for the ego to overcome this psychic danger, the leap from this state to the next is no longer felt as an activity of the ego. Thus the *Dasabhumi-sutra* metaphorically speaks of the transition from the seventh stage, "Far-going," to the eighth, "Immovable," as follows: A sleeping man sees himself in a dream trying desperately to cross a raging torrent and to reach the yonder shore. His hopeless attempt awakens him. Once awakened, he finds himself free from all dis-ease (*duhkhas*) of worry, despair, frustration, or agony. The *sutra* describes this experience of *satori*, or awakening as "without merits" (*anabhogatas*).[23] The phrase "without merits" refers to the psychological condition wherein self-realization takes place so as the ego comes to function in an "ex-centric" manner in the service of the Self. Jung refers to this psychological state as "an ego-less mental condition," "consciousness without an ego," or the like, which is also expressed by St. Paul as the state in which "It is no longer I who live, but Christ who lives in me" (*Galatians* 2:20).[24] The *Dasabhumi-sutra* maintains, therefore, that the practice of the ten *paramitas,* or "perfections," in this eighth stage — as well as the last two stages — is carried out in and through the realization of the Buddha's wisdom and compassion. In other words, in these three last stages, the Bodhisattva is in the service of, and in perfect unison with, the spontaneous manifestation of the activity of the Buddha's wisdom and compassion. The expression "without merits" designates this "Self-centric" functioning of the psyche in self-realization.[25]

In the eigth picture, the "Self-centric" functioning of the psyche is symbolized by the empty circle. As mentioned above, the circle in which each of the ten pictures is portrayed represents the ever-present activity of the Buddha-nature, or the Self in which Zen practice is pursued. Therefore, the "empty circle" of the eighth picture can be taken as depicting the fully manifested activity of the Buddha-nature, or the Self, in the conscious life of the practitioner whose ego functions in the service of the Self. This is to say, in this "Self-centric" condition of the psyche, the individual experiences the paradoxical state-process of simultaneous occurrence of emptying-fulfilling, or negating-affirming, in regard to the psychological life. The ego is emptied by the very act of the Self realizing, or fulfilling, its urge. To put it differently, in facing the emptying activity of the Self's urge, the ego is forced endlessly and relentlessly to sacrifice whatever it has achieved. Yet this sacrifice of the ego is, at the same time, the fulfillment of the urge of the Self, or the genuine man.

Accordingly, this ego-sacrifice in the sense of Self-fulfillment must not be confused with ego-dissolution or ego-depotentiation. On the contrary, the integrated ego is strong and flexible enough to develop the attitude of listening in order to function harmoniously with the Self. The ego thus strengthened can function in unison with, and in the service of the Self. Therefore, the word "forgotten" used in Kuo-an's title, "The Ox and the Man both Forgotten," designates the emptying activity of the Buddha-nature, or the Self, which is supraordinate to the function of the ego. Hence, once the "Self-centric" functioning of the psyche takes place, the "ego-centric" functioning of the psyche is "forgotten" or has disappeared. What is overcome is not the ego itself but the function of the ego which is to be characterised as "ego-centric." In Buddhism the term "ego-centric" is used to describe the ego's appropriating orientation which is conditioned by the darkness or ignorance and the egoistic passion of defilement and which, accordingly, obscures the genuine activity of the Buddha-nature. In the Taoist tradition, the word "forgotten" (*wang*) has been used synonymously with *wu-wei*, "non-doing" or "letting something be," or *tsu-jan*, "naturalness" or "being through itself." Therefore, the word "forgotten" indicates the psychological condition of "being emptied" (*kung, sunyata*) wherein the ego is opened to the service of the activity of the Self, the matrix of life.

The last two pictures of Kuo-an's version continue to describe the "Self-centric" functioning of the psyche. For the individuated ego, or the ego functioning in the service of the Self, neither the human world nor the natural world are experienced as alien to itself. Both nature and human activity become authentic to the genuine man. He experiences both as the Buddha-nature realizing itself in different modalities. Psychologically viewed, the experience of the Buddha-nature, or the Self, in nature and human relationships can be understood as paralleling the archetype of the Self which is sometimes associated with synchronistic or parapsychological events. In the *Preface* to the ninth picture, "Returning to the Origin, Back to the Source," Kuo-an states: "From the very beginning, pure and immaculate, the man has never been affected by defilement" (p. 133). This "original so-ness" refers to the universal presence of the activity of the Buddha-nature, or the Self, which realizes itself in and through the receptive, flexible ego. The same idea of "naturalness" is also referred to in the last line of Kuo-an's *Verse*: "Behold the streams flowing whither nobody knows; and the flowers vividly red — for whom are they?" (p. 134). This verse can be translated literally as follows: "The stream flows on its own accord, and the flower is red on its own accord." The Chinese term *tsu*, "of its own accord," is used as a compound, *tsu-jan*, in Taoist thought, meaning "naturalness," occurring as the creative spontaneity of nature, within and without. In other words, *tsu-jan* can be taken psychologically as the living reality of self-realization, or the creative urge of the Self manifesting itself in nature.

The living reality of the Self is also experienced in human affairs as interpersonal relationships. This is the theme of the last picture, in Kuo-an's version entitled "Entering the City with Bliss-bestowing Hands." A common, everyday occurrence is portrayed in which a young man is meeting an old man in the market place. In his *Preface*, Kuo-an states: "Carrying a gourd he [the old man] goes into the market, leaning against a staff he comes home. He is found in company with wine-bibbers and butchers, he and they are all converted into Buddhas" (p. 134).

It should be noted here that the old man depicted in the picture has a belly protruding like that of the so-called laughing Buddha. D.T. Suzuki interprets this emphasis on the belly as showing the significance of "diaphragmatic thinking," or "a sort of 'thinking' which is done with the whole body or the whole 'person.' "[26] This man embodies what Lin-chi (d. 866) calls "the total action of total being."[27] A man who "thinks" thus goes anywhere he likes and makes all sorts of friends as a manifested activity of *sunyata*, which is symbolized by the gourd he carries. In other words, this man is the genuine man in and through whom self-realization or emptying/fulfilling activity of the Buddha-nature, takes place. Tsu-te, the author of the *Six Oxherding Pictures*, depicts in the last, sixth, picture the life of the genuine man, or the Self, as a person who can function as a total being, or the Self, by playfully assuming any *samsaric* form of existence, depending on the circumstances in which he finds himself.[28] This playfulness is, psychologically understood, "an ego-less" or the "Self-centric" condition of the psyche wherein self-realization takes place. In Buddhism, it is the play of the Bodhisattva who, out of selfless compassion, mingles with sentient beings in suffering in order to liberate them. In this manner, this last picture merges with the first picture on a different level of consciousness.

Psychologically, the *Oxherding Pictures* can be taken as portraying in an art form what Jung calls individuation. Our study, employing Jung's concepts and methodology, has afforded us a psychological understanding of Zen *satori* (enlightenment) in terms of self-realization, or the urge of the Self to realize itself. The essential feature of *satori* does not consist in ego-transcendence or ego-negation, but rather in a life-long process which demands that the ego make ceaseless efforts towards the integration of the unconscious contents. The ego thus enriched and strengthened through the assimilation of the unconscious is freed from "egocentric" ways of functioning, which are conditioned by the darkness of ignorance and passion. Consequently, the ego can attain an attitude which allows it to function in an "ex-centric" manner in perfect unison with, and in the service of, the Self. This state can be designated as "Self-centric." Lin chi calls it "the total action of the total being," or the Self realizing itself in its totality.

REFERENCES

1. J. Jacobi, *The Way of Individuation*, trans. R.F.C. Hull (New York: Harcourt, Brace & World, Inc., 1967), p. 72. J. Henderson, "The Jungian Orientation to Eastern Religion" (taped lecture. Los Angeles: C.G. Jung Institute, 1975). See M. Miyuki, "A Jungian Approach to the Pure Land Practice of *Nien-fo*," *The Journal of Analytical Psychology* (London: The Society of Analytical Psychology), Vol. 24, no. 3 (July 1980), pp. 265-274.

2. This article is a further elaboration of the paper entitled *"Selbstverwirklichung* in the Ten Oxherding Pictures," presented at the Eighth International Congress of International Association for Analytical Psychology. San Francisco. September, 1980.

3. Various numbers of the *Verses* which accompany *The Oxherding Pictures* are found in the *Zoku zokyo* as follows: Kuo-an's *Prefaces and Verses to The Ten Oxherding Pictures* (1. 2, 113, pp. 459a-406b and 1. 2. 116, pp. 489a-b); Pu-ming's *Verses to The Ten Oxherding Pictures* (1. 2. 113, pp. 461a-462a), which are followed by those of many other masters who also wrote their *Verses* to accompany the pictures used by Pu-ming. Hence, the popularity of Pu-ming's version is undeniable. The last of these masters is Chu-che, who also wrote the ten verses to *The White Ox Pictures* (1. 2. 113, pp. 470b-471a). There are also two other masters' *Verses to The Oxherding Pictures*; namely, the *Verses for The Six Oxherding Pictures*, composed by Tsu-te Hui-hui of the twelfth century (1. 2. 116, pp. 489b-490a) and the *Verses for The Four Oxherding Pictures* (1. 2. 137, pp. 210a-b) by Hsueh-ting, a contemporary of Kuo-an. These different *Verses*, composed by the five Zen Masters, to *The Oxherding Pictures* of various numbers are translated into English by Zenkei Shibayama. See *The Zen Oxherding Pictures*. Commentaries by Zenkei Shibayama and Paintings by Gyokusei Jikihara (Osaka: Sogensha, 1975). For an English translation and exposition of *The Six Oxherding Pictures*, see Z. Shibayama, *The Six Oxherding Pictures*, trans. Sumiko Kudo (Kyoto?): The Nissha Printing Co., Ltd. No Date).

4. For the English translation of Kuo-an's and Pu-ming's texts, I have used D.T. Suzuki's translation in his *Manual of Zen Buddhism* (London: Rider and Company, 1950), pp. 127-144. Suzuki's translation of Kuo-an's text with his discussion is also found in his article, "The Awakening of a New Consciousness in Zen," in *Man and Transformation*. Bollingen Series xxx 5 (New York: Pantheon Books, 1964), pp. 179-202. For another translation and discussion of Kuo-an's version, see M.H. Treavor, tr. *The Ox and His Herdsman: A Chinese Zen Text* (Tokyo: Hoduseido Press, 1969).

5. Yanagida Seizan, "Ni-hon zen no toku-shoku" (Characteristics of Japanese Zen), in Ogisu Jundo, ed., *Zen to ni-hon buk-ka no sho mon-dai* (Problems of Zen and Japanese Culture) (Kyoto, Heirakuji shoten, 1969), pp. 79-84.

6. *Zoku zokyo* 1. 2. 113, p. 459a.

7. Z. Shibayama, *The Six Oxherding Pictures*, pp. 3-4.

8. See D.T. Suzuki, *Studies in Zen* (London: Rider and Company, 1955), p. 48.

9. Chih-yen, *Hua-yen ching K'ung-mu chang* (The Essentials of the *Hua-yen Sutra*), Taisho 45, p. 549b-c.

10. C.G. Jung, "On 'The Tibetan Book of the Great Liberation'," *Psychology and Religion: West and East. The Collected Works of C.G. Jung* (hereafter abridged as CW) 11 (New York: Pantheon Books, Inc., 1958), par. 774.

11. C.G. Jung, *The Practice of Psychotherapy*, CW 16, par. 366.

12. C.G. Jung, *Two Essays on Analytical Psychology*, CW 7, par 266.

13. E.F. Edinger, *Ego and Archetype* (Baltimore, Maryland: Penguin Books, Inc., 1973), p. 104.

14. C.G. Jung, "Transformation Symbolism in the Mass," CW 11, par. 391.

15. C.G. Jung, *Memories, Dreams, Relfections*, recorded and edited by Aniela Jaffe: Trans. Richard and Clara Winston (New York: Pantheon Books, 1961), p. 3.

16. See footnote 11 above.

17. C.G. Jung, *Aion*, CW 9, ii, par, 123.

18. C.G. Jung, "On the Nature of the Psyche," *The Structure and Dynamics of the Psyche*, CW 8, par. 405.

19. Edward F. Edinger, *Ego and Archetype*, p. 5.

20. Ibid., p. 188. For a discussion on the mandala symbolism of the ternary process and quaternary completion in the major teachings of Buddhism, see M. Miyuki, "The Ideational Content of the Buddha's Enlightenment as *Selbstverwirklichung*" (see present volume).

21. See D.T. Suzuki, *Studies in Zen*, p. 48.

22. *The Dasabhumisvaro nama mahayanasutram*, Edited Pyuko Kindo (Tokyo: The Daijyo Bukkyo Kenkyu-kai, 1936), p. 119. The first seven stages are the stages in which the Bodhisattva is said not to be completely free from *klesa* or defilement. The finality of the Bodhisattva's realization in the eighth stage is also suggested by its name, i.e., "Immovable (*acala*), which indicates that the Bodhisattva firmly establishes himself in Buddha's wisdom and compassion.

23. Ibid., p. 135.

24. See C.G. Jung, "On 'The Tibetan Book of the Great

Liberation'." CW 11, par 744. Also see C.G. Jung's "Foreword to 'Introduction to Zen Buddhism'." CW, par. 890.

25. The ninth stage is called "Excellent Wisdom" (*sadhumati*). At this stage the Bodhisattva attains the four wisdoms of non-hinderances by which he can preach the profound *dharma* of the Buddha. The tenth stage is called "*Dharma*-Cloud" (*dharma-magha*). At this stage of the final realization, the Bodhisattva bestows Buddha's wisdom and compassion, or an abundance of *dharma* like rain on all sentient beings in order to liberate them from the *samsaric* existence of suffering and sorrow.

26. D.T. Suzuki, "The Awakening of a New Consciousness in Zen," in *Man and Transformation*, p. 201.

27. Lin-chi, *Chen-chou Lin-chi Hui-chao ch'an-shih y-lu* (The Dialogues of the Zen Master Lin-chi Hui-chao), Taisho 47, p. 501b.

28. See Z. Shibayama, *The Six Oxherding Pictures*, pp. 44.

THE OXHERDING PICTURES
OF ZEN BUDDHISM:
A Commentary
By J. Marvin Spiegelman

Preliminary

When I first happened upon the Ten Oxherding Pictures, in *Manual of Zen Buddhism* by D.T. Suzuki (1960), it was as if I had found a great treasure, a visual representation of the process of individuation in succinct, powerful form. I immediately thought of the series of pictures from the *Rosarium Philosophorum*, the German alchemical pictures which Jung (1946) had used so brilliantly and profoundly to illustrate the transference. He showed, thereby, that the underlying meaning of the transference was the individuation process.

It was 1960, and I was back in the United States, in the midst of the hurly-burly of earning a living, being a husband and father, trying to maintain the deep inner connection with the soul which was so nourished by my years of training at the C.G. Jung Institute in Zurich. Sometimes I felt that I was not at all doing what I had been trained to do and found it beyond my powers to connect the introverted existence I had grown used to with the requirements of adaptation to work and life in extraverted America. The Oxherding Pictures were like a stream opening up in the midst of the dry Southern California desert. I recalled my dream of my psyche opening to the orient (see East and West: A Personal Statement) and once more felt a continuity of process. My own individuation was now proceding onward, despite the appearance of blockage and wrong-turning. Synchronistically, I met my first analysand from the Orient, and my link with the East, particularly with Japan, has not been seriously interrupted ever since.

Some years later, in a seminar, I attempted to present a commentary on these pictures, along with my friend and colleague, Mokusen Miyuki, but found that I could in no way satisfactorily convey my understanding and appreciation of the series, despite my strong desire and an apparently receptive audience. Once more I experienced the gap between a charged and meaningful inner connection and my capacity to link this up with the outer world. This time, however, it was not only my own inner life that was involved, it was the larger interior life of the whole cultural experience of Buddhism which was hard to convey. Within a short time, however, Buddhism burst into California like a great flood, along with the spiritual revolution of the sixties, and soon its general attitudes, tenets and techniques became a part of the general consciousness of spiritually inclined people. A deeper sense of reconciliation of inner and outer, of connection with "the face before you were born," with the Self and its unity, were just as evanescent as ever.

At that time, there appeared a paper by the same great scholar of Buddhism, D.T. Suzuki (1964), "Awakening of a New Consciousness in Zen," which included the Oxherding Pictures, along with a brief commentary. When I saw how even the great Suzuki struggled to convey his comprehension of Enlightenment and the difficulties with it, I was consoled. I was startled to discover, however, that my own understanding of the pictures differed in some measure from his. Who was I to have a view about such a work at all? I realized, then, that I was using the pictures as a guideline, a source, and from a *psychological* point of view and not as a scholar, a religious partisan (Buddhist), nor one thoroughly steeped spiritually and culturally in such matters. I shall have occasion, in what follows, to mention these differences of interpretation, but mainly I shall be continuing the process of my own use of these treasures from China and Japan. I shall, therefore, be thinking of *individuation*, rather than *Enlightenment*, will be experiential rather than scholarly, Californian and personal, rather than Oriental and transpersonal. I do attempt, however, to be comparative and to establish links with the scholarly and transpersonal.

Before I turn to the pictures themselves, I wish to continue this explanation of how I arrived at even the possibility of such an endeavor. In 1967, while at work on a fictional account of the individuation process in various cultures and climes, I was inspired to write a story of such a process using those same Oxherding Pictures. In April 1967, on Buddha's birthday, I began such a story, called *The Ronin*, which was my best attempt to both live through and convey the individuation theme as shown in the pictures. That story became part of a larger work, *The Tree: Tales in Psycho-Mythology*, (1982, Falcon Press, Phoenix Az.) as I mention in East and West: A Personal Statement. *The Ronin* is included in this book as another way of communicating what it is that we are about in the individuation process or the journey towards Enlightenment.

This fictional account was followed up by another story of individuation seen from pictures, this time from those almost-as-fascinating images in Kundalini Yoga, commented upon by Arthur Avalon (1918) in *The Serpent Power*. This story, in contrast to the Buddhist spiritual warrior in *The Ronin*, is from a Hindu woman's point of view. It is called *Maya, the Yogini*. These two tales, plus the use of the *Rosarium* pictures of alchemy (in the story of *The African*) in that same book, *The Tree*, began to satisfy my quest for a kind of *ecumenical* individuation and spiritual journey with the use of pictures. Finally, it took three volumes to truly bring together the many-fold stories and variations into one larger Kabbalistic, Taoistic, Buddhistic, Christian, Pagan whole (1975, 1982, 1984 ff).

So continued my desire to explicate or communicate this hard-to-describe process to a larger public. I grew to realize that this same effort at communication was still part of my own process of linking up this strange inner unity and multiplicity to the outer world with its equally strange unity and multiplicity. I thought that my efforts could come to rest, but this was not to be the case. The vicissitudes of publishing (rejection, then acceptance but the publisher going bankrupt), continued the same adventure but now in the outer world. So the same conflict of inner and outer, East and West, introversion and extraversion, spirit and body, continued, now embodied in my "child" (the three books of fiction) being able to walk around on its own in the world.

It was not until 1982 that this long-term repeat of the blockage of 1959-60 was opened up once more. Again, the opening came from the East, from Japan. My colleague, Dr. Mokusen Miyuki, and I were invited to be principal speakers in an East-West Conference taking place in Tokyo and Kyoto. I thus wrote my East-West paper for that conference, speaking around the time, once more, of Buddha's birthday, and enjoyed a totally heart-warming reception from Japanese people. Among my many East-West experiences was contact with a Swiss Catholic Priest who was a scholar of Japanese Buddhism, and a Japanese Protestant

Minister who was about to become a Jungian Analyst! I felt at home.

That same period brought my re-connection with a friend, who had now become a publisher and was interested in bringing out my work, both fiction and non-fiction. And so, the circle (as in Oxherding picture VIII) comes around to its starting point and I once more have the opportunity to sum up and convey what those pictures mean to me. For the last three or four years, I have also lectured on these pictures to candidates in Jungian training, to give them another view of the individuation process, in addition to that shown by Jung's alchemical portrayal. Here ends the *apologia*, that a Westerner might be so audacious as to write a commentary at all!

Introduction

Suzuki (1960 p. 127) tells us that the originals of the pictures we are using were painted by a Zen Master of the Sung dynasty in China, called Kaku-an Shi-en. This same master also authored the remarkable poems and introductory comments which are attached to the pictures. The ones in general use in Japan, however, were painted by Shubun, a contemporary Japanese Zen priest of the fifteenth century. There are other sets of pictures with the same or similar theme, notably those by Seikyo (a contemporary of Kaku-an) and by Jitoku. These latter are notable in that the process ends with the circle, rather than the human reconnection in life as in Kaku-an's and that there is a longer sequence in which the ox undergoes notable whitening. These pictures will be commented upon later on, but here we can only note that the Kaku-an pictures are both more profound, in that they include stages beyond that attainment of wholeness shown by the circle, and that his pictures are more delicate, refined and differentiated. It is particularly remarkable of Kaku-an to have completed such a full task when his contemporaries, and the even later (1585) work of Chu-hung with poems by Pu-ming, are clearly more primitive in conception and execution.

When we compare both sets of pictures with those of the *Rosarium*, we see at once that the Chu-hung and the alchemical series are of similar rough quality, so that Kaku-an's achievement stands out even more. What is suggested by this particular refinement and differentiation of the Zen Master is uncertain. Clearly, he is an inheritor of an already old and revealed tradition with highly differentiated concepts, stages and achievements, whereas the alchemical tradition was usually a hidden one.

Alchemy was in a very different relation to the socially accepted religion of Christianity than the Oxherding pictures was to Buddhism. Whereas the latter explicated the basic tenets and revealed them, alchemy *compensated* the prevailing religion by describing a work in nature and in man, as Jung so eloquently demonstrates. So we have, as we shall see, a remarkably modern and clear presentation of the developmental process in the older commentary by Kaku-an, in contrast to the alchemical work which is abstruse and seemingly more distant to our modern ear, though closer to us in time and culture. Thanks to Jung, however, we can connect these two works, arising in roughly similar times but continents away in space. I believe, however, they are complementary in spirit.

Both series have ten pictures, just as do the Kundalini series, and those of Tarot (at least for the ten Sephiroth of the Kabbalistic Tree of Life; there are additional pictures of course, for their interconnections). Jung informs us (*Vol. 16*, 1946, paragraph 525 and footnote) that ten, the *denarius*, is considered to be a perfect number. The Axiom of Maria, an alchemical formula of wholeness, runs 4,3,2,1, in sequence. The sum of these numbers is ten, which stands for unity on a higher level. This same unity, as Jung explains from the alchemical sources, stands for the *res simplex*, God as an indivisible unity and the monad. God is ten, therefore the beginning and end of all numbers. The archetypal significance of this -- which probably holds for the Oriental psyche as well as the West -- is that of the Self, in Jung's sense, the symbolic representation of that totality. The presentation of exactly ten pictures on both continents, then, portrays and unfolds the nature of that wholeness, which we in the West call God and the East calls Self.

As we look at the structure of the pictures themselves, we immediately note that the *Rosarium* images have no outer frame at all, in contrast to those of the Oxherding series. Those of Chu-hung have a very clear square to contain the series, while Kaku-an uses both an outer square for each picture and an inner circle to contain the content and action. Does this perhaps also reflect that the Oriental way is "contained" and part of the prevailing religious collective, whereas the alchemical images are, indeed, outside the pale, not contained in the prevalent religious structure? I think that this is true, since the very beginning of the alchemical series shows the problem and presentation of the "vessel" itself: a Mercurial fountain and a basin into which the waters flow and from which they arise. The framing is provided by symbols such as the snakes spitting smoke, the stars, sun and moon and not simply lines. We are faced with the problem of the vessel, the container, right away. Where does the transformation take place? In matter, in chemicals, in people, in nature? No person is shown in the *Rosarium* at the outset, only the attempt at discovering the basis of the transformation process itself. In the Oxherding series, we are immediately confronted with a person, the young man, and know at once that his dilemma and search is at the core of the issue. He is the one to be transformed. So, then, the structure or frame -- Buddhism and meditation -- is already known. How different from the "experiments" of alchemy!

As we consider, next, this issue of the appearance of people in the pictures, we again perceive a central difference. The human being is presented at the outset, and continually in the Eastern series, with his absence being particularly notable and significant in the last-but-one picture and its predecessor. In the *Rosarium* series, after the initial image which is concerned with the vessel, all pictures portray the vicissitudes of the person, but as a pair, male and female, king and queen. In the latter, the entire series is concerned with the differentiation and union of these two alchemical figures, resulting in a oneness, a hermaphrodite, at the end. With the Oxherding series, however, we are involved with one person, an ordinary young man, until he vanishes temporarily, with good reason, only to emerge at the end, changed, transformed, old, but full of the life and vitality of the Enlightened person.

We can clearly see the complementary nature of the process as grasped by the two world-views. In the one, contained and understood in the religious collective of the day, there is the task of the ordinary person to achieve Enlightenment. In the other -- secret, apart and even unknowing of what one is about -- there gradually emerges a knowledge that the person is a vessel for the union of opposites, and that, finally, individuation is a process which requires human relationship. Jung makes much of this relationship requirement in his commentary, so that it is particularly notable how the two sets end. In the West there is a unity, one androgynous creature. In the East there is the lonely man, after a long work with himself, finally joining other people in ordinary life (the wine-bibbers, etc.) At the end, he even meets someone who looks remarkably like he, himself, looked at the outset.

One gets images from such presentations. In the East, the seeker meditates, alone. He seeks advice from a Master, may even live in a monastery, but ultimately he meditates alone. In the West, one seeks psychotherapy, and the process of individuation is very much felt in the context of the analytical relationship. Indeed, the very content of this individuation process in psychotherapy reveals itself -- unexpectedly from the point of view of the founders of this discipline -- in the relationship itself, the transference.

So man alone transforms himself and comes back into the world; and man finds himself in relation with another and thus unifies the fragmentation of his soul. Complementary, indeed! It seems particularly striking that the psyche, East and West, was presenting itself in this complementary fashion around the same time in the fifteenth century in China and Japan, and in the sixteenth century in Europe. Was there a similar "renaissance" of the spirit being worked on in both areas of the world? And now, more than four hundred years later, when we compare, unite and further develop the spirits of the East and West, are we in the midst of another "renaissance," presaging world unity?

If we look a little further into this role of the person/persons in the two sets of pictures, we see that in the East there is no female. In the West, the feminine is present from the outset, in the symbolic form of vessel, of moon, etc., and then quite literally throughout in the form of the queen. In the East, no woman at all. How many women meditated, visited gurus, sought enlightenment? Some, of course, since there have been Zen priestesses, for example, for a very long time. It was mostly a man's work, however. But was alchemy so different? There was Maria Prophetissa, of course, and the profound influence of her "axiom," but were there female alchemists? One doesn't know, but Jung intuits and I think rightly, that there must have been some form of *soror mystica*, a feminine partner who was something additional to the projection of the male alchemist's own anima. But we know nothing of this. In the pictures, however, the feminine is clearly personified in the West, but in the East, it is all background. It is a circle, it is nature, it is the animal, it is both the source and goal of the work.

In the East it is assumed, but not personified. In the West it is personified and consciously united with. Perhaps it is part of the West's gift to have the feminine as an equal, participatory partner and that a future set of pictures, East and West, will have the personal feminine and her process as much a part of the work as is archetypally portrayed in these two sets.

It would be a mistake, however, to simply call both sets just a part of the masculine individuation process or search for Enlightenment. They are, rather, portraits of the "masculine," not men, just as the portrayal of nature, circle, etc. are of the "feminine" and not women. We are witness to the growth and differentiation of the archetypal opposites, of king and queen, and not just those of our ordinary egos. Both sets give us Enlightenment about ourselves, male and female, masculine and feminine, and their union.

We can turn, now, to the individual pictures of the Eastern series, to concentrate on their sequence, and only occasionally remark on the comparison with the West. Before we do so, however, one should note that another Eastern series, that of the *Kundalini*, shares characteristics of the West, in that the male and female, god and goddess, are part of almost every picture, ultimately leading to a genderless union at the highest level. In this, it is like the West. But in *Kundalini*, male, as form, only gradually grows in power and signficance, whereas female, as energy and power, gradually differentiates and becomes civilized and spiritualized. In East and West, we have glimpses of the need to civilize and differentiate, as well as to redeem and recover our origins in nature and instinct. But the Oxherding series departs from *Kundalini*, just as Buddhism did from Hinduism.

We shall present Kaku-an's commentary and poem, for each picture, followed by a discussion of their meaning to us.

Picture One: Searching for the Ox

The beast has never gone astray, and what is the use of searching for him? The reason the oxherd is not on intimate terms with him is that the oxherd himself has violated his own inmost nature. The beast is lost, for the oxherd has himself been led out of the way, through his deluding senses. His home is receding farther away from him, and byways and crossways are ever confused. Desire for gain and fear of loss burn like fire; ideas of right and wrong spring up like a phalanx.

> Alone in the wilderness, lost in the jungle,
>   the boy is searching, searching!
>
> The swollen waters, the faraway mountains,
>   and the unending path;
>
> Exhausted and in despair, he knows not
>   where to go,
>
> He only hears the evening cicadas singing
>   in the maple woods.

How modern sound these words of Kaku-an! How strange that our ear can hear the plaint of the contemporary person who has lost his soul and is in search of it, here and there and everywhere. No longer believing in God, nor man, nor "isms," the person described in Jung's works as "A Modern Man in Search of a Soul" is cut off from himself, estranged from his own depths, not knowing where to turn. So, too, is the oxherd, of four hundred years ago, lost.

But what is this ox that he is searching for? Suzuki tells us that it is the mind, or heart, or better yet, the Self. It is that Self of the Buddhist, or that Self of the Jungians, which is the center and higher authority within, or the totality of his being, which is portrayed here as an animal. Suzuki also tell us (1964, p. 198) that the ox comes from the *niu* in Chinese, or *ushi* in Japanese, which designates the bovine family generally; it is ox and cow and bull, of no specific gender. It is the sacred animal in India and this compared to the Self, or, as we in the West might say, the God within.

What Suzuki does not say, but perhaps those who are more familiar with the symbolism in other cultures can realize, is that the Self here appears as an animal, just as the Divine appears represented as an animal in many traditions, even Christianity (Jesus as the Lamb, for instance, and the evangelists with animal symbols as representative of them). When we come to discuss pictures IV to VI we shall see how it is that we can have a different view than Suzuki of this matter, but here we are in agreement: the ox equals Self.

How can it be that the young man (ourselves) is estranged from the Self, himself. "The beast has never gone astray," says the text, and Suzuki agrees. The original Self, or home, is one that we have never left, but "owing to our intellectual delusions, we are led to imagine (the Self) has disappeared from our sight. Searching for the lost is a great initial error we all commit, which makes us think we are finally awakened to a new consciousness."

Our psychological consciousness may help us understand this paradox. The original Self, of course, is always there. It is the "face before we were born," it is the potential wholeness from which we come at the outset of existence and to which we both return and achieve. But it is also something from which we can be estranged, just as we, in the modern day, can be estranged from our animal nature, as is implied by the Oxherding pictures. Full of our modern rationalist delusions, the belief that reason and external evidence provide the only truth, we are cut off from our animal wisdom, our instincts. We thus endure a kind of deadness, cut off from vitality and spontaneity, or else we are split and experience mind and body as apart, separated.

The wonder is that this dilemma can be expressed with such poetry and accuracy in the pictures and words of an alien culture of more than 400 years ago! Can it be that the Chinese and Japanese of the fifteenth century, whom we usually believe to be more whole and united than we of the scientific present day, were also afflicted with our disease? It seems to be. Not only that, but there is indication that such a struggle comes from an older tradition, that these poems and pictures are already part of the institution of healing, just as is modern psychotherapy. This tells us that our perceived understanding of the predicament of modern man is not exclusively modern at all. In every age, perhaps, there is the tendency of the psyche to dissociate itself, to spontaneously produce "neurosis," not as a consequence of external events alone, but as a result of the need of the soul itself to differentiate further, to acquire more consciousness. Von Franz describes just such a condition in her *Introduction to the Interpretation of Fairy Tales* (1970). Splitting and fragmentation can occur in the larger culture, just as it can in the individual, as the need to develop further, to fulfill that same potential of greater consciousness which was there in the beginning.

Is it not also possible that the China and Japan of the fifteenth century were also in a condition similar to that of Europe, undergoing an upheaval, in which the order of the middle ages was breaking up?

In any case, the words here speak to our modern condition very well. Nowadays, we have more than ever "gone astray" and we are not on good terms with our inmost nature. Kaku-an tells us that we are lost because of our "deluding senses." What deludes us is the act of giving total authority to what our five senses present to us from without, or even from within, and we do not open ourselves to mystery, imagination, to the images which embellish and enrich and even go beyond the information presented from those same senses. So we are ever further away from the experience of wholeness and aliveness, the sense of wonder without which life is a meaningless round of drudgery.

Kaku-an tells us the psychic content of such a soul who is confused on the way, knows he is lost, but has no sense of where to find the path. "Desire for gain and fear of loss burn like fire, ideas of right and wrong spring up like a phalanx." Again what an insight! Desire, and competition and yearning for material gain is our plague. We are a wild, undisciplined animal who lives in an urban jungle, far from home. Along with the plague of desire comes a judge with rigid views of right and wrong, ever evaluating and condemning. Self and others are found wanting, we receive no compassion, enjoy no rest. Is this not a poetic rendering of what the first modern psychologist diagnosed? Id versus Superego, said Freud; wish and desire versus guilt and judgment. Such is the kingdom of our discontent, such is the pessimistic struggle for which there is only consciousness as a valued outcome, a sweet reason of awareness in the midst of pain.

But the Oxherding pictures and Zen promise more than a diagnosis of despair and hopelessness, even here in the first picture. The "more" is found in the poem, the soft words of which picture for us the condition and the hope as well. The poet tells us of the lostness, and the searching, the unending searching. He tells us of the exhaustion and despair and the not knowing where to go. But he also tells us that the lost boy hears "the evening cicadas singing in the maple woods."

What is this cicada if not the voice of nature herself, chirping her age-old tune of joy and happiness, of oneness and harmony with herself. The *Oxford Dictionary* tells us that the cicada is a "homopterous insect," which means that its wings are of uniform texture, patterned and harmonious. Our western version of the cicada is the cricket, which the *Standard Dictionary of Folklore* (1949) tells us was "much esteemed in antiquity," and had the quality of bringing good and bad fortune, depending upon one's attitude toward it. It was a prophet (of rain, death, or the approach of an absent lover), a nostrum in healing, and a personification of the spirit of the house, especially at the hearth. Thus the cicada is a symbol for potential order, for harmony, for the oneness or union of animal and man (insect and warming center of civilized condition). Depending upon one's attitude, we are thereby in tune with time (prophecy), love, renewal and even healed. Our suffering youth, then, in hearing the cicada, is given an intuition, a promise of wholeness in tiny, hardly visible form. His suffering is not just that of endless despair, but he can perceive the possiblity of hope as well.

We must not forget the other imagery of the poem and what our modern psychology can tell us about it. "Swollen waters": a symbol of the filled unconscious, ready to disgorge its contents, frightening, but promising renewal. "Faraway mountains": a symbol of the individuation process, that struggle to reach the higher vision, to master oneself and touch the place where God lives, atop mountains; for where God lives, there is higher consciousness and greater vision. And finally, the "unending path": the ancient symbol of the "way," the process of moving Godward, of the seeking of the treasure hard to obtain.

All this does the poet tell us and all this does he convey in that oriental fashion, with an image, with a word, a kind of *haiku* of the spiritual path.

Picture II: Seeing the Traces

By the aid of the sutras and by inquiring into the doctrines, he has come to understand something, he has found the traces. He now knows that vessels, however varied, are all of gold, and that the objective world is a reflection of the Self. Yet, he is unable to distinguish what is good from what is not, his mind is still confused as to truth and falsehood. As he has not yet entered the gate, he is provisionally said to have noticed the traces.

By the stream and under the trees, scattered
are the traces of the lost;

The sweet-scented grasses are growing thick--
did he find the way?

However remote over the hills and faraway
the beast may wander,

His nose reaches the heavens and none can
conceal it.

Kaku-an now tells us how one can procede on the path to spiritual growth, to Enlightenment, to one's reconciliation with one's self when one is confused and tormented. Given one's ignorance, one studies the sutras and enquires into the doctrines. We must then, in our modern dilemma, which seeks the psychotherapeutic route to Enlightenment or individuation, read the Bible -- Jewish and Christian -- the Koran, as well as the true sutras of the East. Thereby, says Kaku-an, will we come to "understand something," we will find the traces. "The traces of what," we may ask? Why the traces of the ox, the divine spirit, the Self which has been apprehended by many in the past, and has left its deposits in the great books, the holy texts, the commentaries. There, at least, we may begin to get a glimpse of how others saw it, of how the divine has manifested itself in the cultures and peoples of other times and places, as well as the culture into which were born, and of whose mysteries and truths we have grown tired and can not abide. Seen another way, the mysteries of all of these are unfathomable to us because we have not yet, or can no longer, grasp them as a living experience.

Still, says Kaku-an, the sutras, the texts, can help us find the traces. Through such study and intellectual attention we can at least come to comparative truths. We can discover that "vessels, however varied, are all of gold." That is to say, we can realize that all religions, all systems which pursue the manifestation of the numinous, of God or the Self, contain a seed or expression of that divine spark which touched the writers and seekers. All containers, all theories, are valuable and holy. And, are we but wise enough to grasp it, we can see that no vessel is the only one made of gold. No religion or creed can rightly claim to be the true and exclusive carrier of the divine. If all vessels are of gold, then no vessel is particularly golden. Yet each vessel, when one is inside it, contains the golden, and sometimes, when that Self speaks through its imagery, through its words and experience, it would seem to be the only one, the particular and amazing. When God speaks to me, I feel that my soul is His beloved, that He speaks only to me, and it is hard for me to know that He does, indeed, speak only to me when He talks to me, but that He has many other lovers as well! And He speaks to them in strange tongues, and sometimes in ways which seem anathema to me. So, if God speaks in Sanskrit and Chinese and Japanese, as well as Hebrew and Greek, Latin and Arabic, German and English, well then, the many tongues are relative. But that is for the most modern day, the day that Suzuki, too, speaks of (1964, p. 198), that time when the world is "becoming one, as it should, and the distinction of East and West is disappearing, though slowly." This day, our day, is not that of Kaku-an, yet he is like us when he knows that all vessels are of gold.

Kaku-an also knows, in this second picture, that the seeker will discover through the sutras, that the "objective world is a reflection of the Self." Yes, we can discover that the same world which deceived us with its multiplicity and variety, with its unnourishing prescriptions, with its facts which offended us, is also a representation of that Self which we are seeking. God's body is "out there" in the world for all to see. The divine is all that mess and confusion, hatred and division, as well as the wonder and love and harmony. What, now; is that all we have found through our study? No, says Kaku-an, no, indeed. For we still cannot distinguish "what is good from what is not," what is true and what is false. We have learned something, but we still do not know the truth of thinking and the values of feeling. We are not yet, in short, in touch with our *own* truth, our *own* values, our *own* Self. We know the languages that God has spoken in the past, but we do not yet know His own to us. We have seen traces but have not yet experienced the Being itself. And now when we speak of God as "He," we think, most modernly, that *ushi* and *niu* are oxes in the sense of gender-free, not castrated; that the divine transcends role and sex, even animal and human! But, as we have not yet entered the gate, have not yet had our own experience of the divine, we can only say that we have "noticed the traces."

The poem leads us in a somewhat different direction. Suzuki tells us that there is nowhere that the *kokoro* is not. "We are always in it, we are it." There is nowhere to seek, nowhere to hide, because "all our running can never be outside the *kokoro* itself." Thus the Self is everywhere we look, and everywhere we do not look, for we are in the Self, and are the Self, and as a later picture advises us, it was silly for us to seek in the first place. But seek we must, because we are unhappy, and because, (and here is where, perhaps, we part from the wisdom of Suzuki and rely on psychological knowledge) this same Self wanted us to do so. Perhaps God Himself, without even being aware of it, cast us out so that we could bring Him back information about Himself. He had everything, it seems, except a partner He could talk to. The Angels only echoed (except for the Devil) and maybe He got bored. The paradox of the Fortunate Fall is one instance; without our fall there would have been no great mystery of redemption. Another is that perhaps there is a natural tendency, i.e. the division within Nature itself, seeking, as we noted from von Franz earlier on, to enhance its own knowledge, to increase consciousness for its own sake. In any event, as Suzuki insists, "there is nothing that can hide him." All that hides him is that we have not yet experienced him.

Perhaps we have to wander by the stream and under the trees, lose ourselves in the sweet palm-grasses of the swamps of our desire and fantasy, in order to begin to reach him. No matter where we go, to whatever theory or belief, or to every abstruse and deviant sect, however wrong-headed we find it, the ox is there. Suzuki, once more, says that when nothing can hide the ox, "It is we who shut our own eyes and pitifully bemoan that we cannot see anything (1964, p. 199)." This is surely true, because the nose reaches the heavens and none can conceal it. And yet, how is it that this same beast eludes us in our own experience? How is it that we must make great effort, even despair at length, before we can go beyond the traces? Is it not because this self-same ox wants us to do so? Does he not require us to pursue, to sweat and to struggle, so that our finding will make the grasses even sweeter, the hills even grander? In the reaching of the nose into the heavens, does the ox not show us the way to search?

And now, indeed, we know that the ox not only is hard to find, but is everywhere, and not only is he beyond our reach, but he wants us to reach him, and without our attempt there is nothing. For even if we had it all along, perhaps there was no one there to know that we had it, and this, indeed, is what the ox desires. Yes, we have desire and ignorance, and perhaps the ox, too, has desire and ignorance? Suzuki would say no, and so would the religions of the West, but perhaps one can conjecture the psychological possibility without disrespect.

But we are only at Picture II and to speculate so is merely to argue with the sutras, merely to note the vessels without actually experiencing the ox. We are still in the state of "Seeing the Traces."

Picture III: Seeing the Ox

The boy finds the way by the sound he hears: he sees thereby into the origin of things, and his senses are in harmonious order. In all his activites, it is manfestly present. It is like the salt in water and the glue in color. (It is there though not distinguishable as an individual entity.) When the eye is properly directed, he will find that it is no other than himself.

On a yonder branch perches a nightingale
cheerfully singing;

The sun is warm, and a soothing breeze
flows, on the bank the willows are green;

The Ox is there all by himself, nowhere
is he to hide himself;

The splendid head decorated with stately
horns -- what painter can reproduce him?

Now, at last, after wandering and not knowing, after reading and studying and reflecting, we go beyond the traces, we come to the experience itself. This, says Suzuki (1964 p. 199), is "the awakening of 'a new consciousness'; it is the finding of the precious animal which is no other than the man himself." But this is not a new finding, it was there all along. It is there in all his activities, everything the seeker does. It is not distinguishable (the salt in water and glue in color) from the surroundings, it is that quality which is inherent in all.

Well, our oxherd knew this from his reading and studying, how is it different now? It is different in that he knows it is himself, or better, his Self, and he knows it through experience. Now he knows it by the "sound he hears," not by what he reads. He listens, it seems. Does he hear the voice of God? Does the Self speak to him personally now, just to him and to no other? Does he now begin to hear his own language, the words of his own being, calling him from within, just as he was *seeking, seeking* without? I think so, particularly when Kaku-an tells us: "When the eye is properly directed, he will find that it is no other than himself."

So, Kaku-an sheds the light that the eye must look in the proper place. Is that not into one's being, one's own fantasies and dreams, affects and strivings? Was it not the ox itself that was driving him to the ox? Once more we think so, for how else can one know the Self unless one knows the self? How can we learn the nature of the totality unless we know our own? And there he is, in the picture, revealed.

What is it that is revealed? The poet speaks of the "splendid head decorated with stately horns." Indeed "what painter can reproduce him?" He wears the beautiful crown of the divine, the horns of grandeur, and there is no way to show his image. This reminds us of the Hebrew word of Torah, enjoining us to produce no graven image of the divine. We are commanded not to, nor to utter His name, for there is no image, there is no word that can encompass this grandeur and wonder and totality. Can the part truly grasp the whole, or render it? Certainly not -- but we must try.

What is it, then, that is revealed here in the picture? No grand head, but a homely behind! No kingly spiritual crown nor impressive sound of the voice, but the vulnerable place of man and beast, our hind-end from which come our excreta, our rejected and unused, that of which we are unconscious. It is our shadow, as Jung says, our own dark side. Is this not so when we truly undertake the voyage of discovery of ourselves? Is it not our own shadows and darkness that is first revealed? This is the wisdom that the artist sees, when the poet looks elsewhere. One voice knows what the other does not.

The rear end we discover, however, is not only our own, which we apprehend all too painfully and sorrowfully, but that of the Self itself. This ox, after all, is not only our own personal ox, but the collective ox, the common content of the soul of us all. And here the Master Kaku-an shows us truly and intuitively that it is the dark side of God that reveals itself to us. All the sutras, all the books, all the commandments, products of many minds, many years, many devotions, show us the whole story, but they cleanse, too, their own darkness, and it is hidden from us. It is only in our own struggle, our own pain of dry meditation, of anger at pain and discomfort, of bleak dreams and disgusting images that we come to our darkness and, at last, the darkness of the divine as well. "The dark night of the soul," another seeker tells us, is essential before we can find the light. So suggests this picture, too.

All the same, however, we have at last found the ox. Once seeing him, once knowing that he arises from our inner search, our reflection and meditation, our fantasy and dream, we can then know that the "sun is warm, and a soothing breeze blows." The willows are green and the nightingale sings, cheerfully, for nature is in harmony with the divine, indeed is the divine. We, at last, see our nature, understand that what we share with all the animals and plants is a cleansing process, that we all partake in materiality and unknowingness. This realization, a gift to humans alone, is the source of our spiritual struggle and path. No body, no true spirit; no shadow, no true light; no dark side of God, no light side either. Hard to understand, hard to accept (as we shall see even with Suzuki presently), but there for us to see. The artist and the poet, inspired, tells us the truth.

Picture IV: Catching the Ox

Long lost in the wilderness, the boy has at last found the ox and his hands are on him. But, owing to the overwhelming pressure of the outside world, the ox is hard to keep under control. He constantly longs for the old sweet-scented field. The wild nature is still unruly, and altogether refuses to be broken. If the oxherd wishes to see the ox completely in harmony with himself, he has surely to use the whip freely.

With the energy of his whole being, the boy
has at last taken hold of the ox:

But how wild his will, how ungovernable
his power!

At times he struts up a plateau,

When lo! he is lost again in a misty unpenetrable
mountain pass.

The hands of the youth are now upon the ox and the task of training and discipline is upon us. Oh, how our desires are primitive and unruly! Oh, how our laziness and the hugging of our primitivity captures us. Our wild nature is unruly and refuses to be broken, indeed. But, is this only our own nature that is so resistive? Suzuki thinks so. He thinks that "Pictures IV, V, and VI are misleading. It is really not the animal but the man himself that needs training and whipping." This is surely true. It is our own animal nature that must be tamed and trained, taught and civilized. But is the picture truly misleading? I think not. The thing that the youth (and we) have gotten our hands upon is the Self, after all, and it is *the* Self, as well as *our* Self. What we have gotten our hands on is the unconscious animal nature of God Himself! It is that in Him which is also unruly, primitive, unconscious, as Jung has shown so powerfully in his work, particularly in *Answer to Job* (1952). We face the paradox that the Self, God, is in all nature, is nature, and partakes both of its great beauty and harmony, and also of its horror, disharmony, and wild disregard. It is the divine in us, indeed, that needs transforming, but it is, at last, the divine itself. This penetrating insight of Jung is the one that is most difficult for many followers of a particular religious system to harmonize for themselves. This is so, whether it is the profound and appreciative Catholic view of a Father White (1961) or even, as here, the view of the great D.T. Suzuki himself.

Why should this perspective be so difficult? I think it is because Jung hit on the peculiarly alchemical character of the work with the psyche, as he found it among those who had lost their belief in the received religious tradition. For them, and for many of the moderns who are "in search of the soul," (See also, *A Modern Jew in Search a Soul*, Falcon Press, winter 1985) the work becomes the redemption of the divine spark in nature, in their own nature, and thus they are in the hidden and mysterious alchemical tradition. So, even here, in a work which is in the heart of the Zen tradition, a leading exponent sees the apparent clarity of the taming of the animal as misleading. It is surely we who need the taming, but as the pictures show, it is the divine itself. So, just as in the *Rosarium* pictures, which Jung used to illustrate individuation and transference, there is the dark power to be reckoned with, larger than ourselves, yet abiding in ourselves. Here, too, there is the dark power to be struggled with, tamed and even whipped, but we must also remember that it is the other half of the longed-for totality.

How remarkable that this hint of the alchemical work (which is even more apparent in the next picture) should reveal itself here, in those times where the same struggle was going on in Europe! There is, one thinks, a synchronicity of the spirit world-wide, when, by dint of meaningful moment or development on a grand plan, an Isaiah and Buddha and a Socrates are contemporaneous, or when an alchemy of the soul occurs in East and West as well.

Kaku-an tells us more about this uncanny ox. He tells us that the animal longs for the old sweet-scented field, that the divine nature and our nature, too, longs to remain unconscious and "natural." Our very attempt at consciousness, at the development of the soul, goes against the grain. Yet, as Jung tells us from alchemy, the work is both against nature, *contra naturam*, and with nature, for it is our own nature itself that drives us to higher consciousness. It is the hidden desire of the ox itself to push us, to seek us, to tame us, and we tame him. This insight is what gives us the permission, allows our audacity to "use the whip freely." Without this insight, without knowing that we are both the one who whips and is whipped, the one who commands and obeys, and in so doing, a pupil and servant of the divine itself -- without this awareness we are lost. Only then can we contain the overweening pride, the hubris of such an act.

How wild the will, how ungovernable the power of this ox! At times, he struts up a plateau. He struts, does he not? He does not walk or run, but he struts. Like some proud and vainglorious cock, he ascends. Here is the source of our own to-be-tamed pride and inflation: it is contained in the divine itself. It is in our nature and His/Her nature. We are chosen ones, or as Suzuki puts it commenting on the previous picture: "Heaven above, heaven below, I alone am the honored one." I am honored because I am addressed, and I can only continue because I honor that which addresses me.

In my struggle, it must be "with the energy of his (my) whole being," it must command all of me. Do I seek my totality? Then I must give my totality. Even when I do, the ox is lost again in the misty, unpenetrable mountain pass. On the path of individuation, upon the ascent to my own highest vision, I lose that divine spark, that source of nature and vitality both within myself and beyond myself. It is gone again, and not to be found. And yet, it appears once more as I start at the beginning, at the perception of that nether end, that bit of untamed nature which is overlooked. Even when I don't look, the ox appears, for once I have glimpsed him, he feels affronted if I neglect him; he comes seeking me, too.

The work is hard, though, and now we lose that initial experience, when we first saw him/her (as in Picture III) and felt the serenity of nature, the nightingale cheerfully singing. The sun may be warm, and the breeze blows, but in this condition we know only struggle and agony and defeat, and achievement and victory and surrender, too.

The work is hard not only because of us and of him, but, says Kaku-an, "owing to the overwhelming pressure of the outside world." What a modern, Enlightened thought is this! How much of our time is spent in adapting, in coping, in facing and struggling with the forces that present themselves in the outer world, when we are oh so eager to struggle within! The God we seek and struggle with within, we sometimes forget, is also there outside. We learned already in the previous pictures that God is in the sutras of tradition and there everywhere, the salt in water. It is outside as well as inside, and when we have discovered the one, we are hounded by the other. So does our work become doubly difficult.

But, no matter, we know, now, the place to look, the place to struggle. For even when the outside world disturbs us, we can look at our own reactions, struggle to be at one with ourselves in relation to these disturbances, so there is always work to be done, something to be tamed, a harmony to seek. We now at last have what we have been looking for.

Picture V: Herding the Ox

When a thought moves, another follows, and then another -- an endless train of thoughts is thus awakened. Through enlightenment all this turns into truth; but falsehood asserts itself when confusion prevails. Things oppress us not because of an objective world, but because of a self-deceiving mind. Do not let the nose string loose, hold it tight, and allow no vacillation.

The boy is not to separate himself with his
    whip and tether,

Lest the animal should wander away into a
    world of defilements;

When the ox is properly tended to, he will
    grow pure and docile;

Without a chain, nothing binding, he will by
    himself follow the oxherd.

Our picture shows the ox, tamed and tempered, dociley following the youth on his tether. The picture shows success, but the words reveal continuing struggle. The thoughts move, falsehood asserts, confusion prevails, the animal wanders away into a world of defilements. No easy task this. Why, we wonder?

Suzuki gives an answer. He says that the "habit of intellectualization, or conceptualization which has been going on ever since his 'loss of innocence,' is extremely difficult to get rid of. The identification is something altogether new in his life. The adjustment will naturally take time." This is helpful and enlightening. It is intellectualization and conceptualization that has cut us off from our own nature. This has resulted in a loss of innocence, a loss of connection with our own nature, which is so difficult to overcome. So, again a paradox emerges: we developed intellectually and conceptually to advance consciousness; but to advance once more in consciousness we must return to our non-thinking nature! That is to say that we no longer identify ourselves solely with our thinking nature. It is this which is problematical. It is not difficult, perhaps, to merely regress and be an animal (though this, too, becomes repugnant to our differentiated functioning), but it is very hard to both return and advance, to recover our nature and tame it.

The difficulty and complexity of this struggle may be the reason why, in Kaku-an's series, six of the ten pictures, sixty per cent of the process, portrays the image of dealing with the animal. Indeed, the name of the series itself, Oxherding Pictures, tells us that the central problem in our individuation is the recovery and taming of our lost natures. Without this -- and this first -- there will be no individuation. Without this, we may perhaps have a bodiless and false spirituality, fit only for those who have no stomach (hara!) for the real thing. Later on, in discussing the final picture, we shall take up this issue of belly and what it means. Here, as we confront the overwhelming importance of the ox, we understand that the main chakra, or orientation of the Zen-Master and those of similar consciousness, is at the belly, the hara where we touch life. It is even where we approach death itself (hara-kiri).

We notice something more about this ox, now, that commands our attention: it has undergone a whitening. From its dark initial condition, it shows itself in a lightened state. That this is not just an accident of printing is shown by the fact that a related series of pictures, that of Seikyo and Jitoku (see Manual of Zen Buddhism, 1960 pp. 127-129 and the subsequent pictures), clearly and explicitly expresses the process of the whitening of the ox. In that series, the whole process ends with an empty circle, the emptiness which Kaku-an (as we shall see) found insufficient to describe the process of Enlightenment. In the Seikyo series, eight out of ten, or eighty percent of the pictures, focus upon this cleansing, differentiating process.

It is from this fact that we can clearly and unequivocally link up the Zen Enlightenment process with the alchemical work as described by Jung. That transformation of *nigredo* (darkening, unconsciousness) to *albedo* (whitening, cleansing) is described by him in detail (in *Psychology and Alchemy*, Vol. 12, 1943, *Mysterium Conjunctionis*, Vol. 14, 1954, and in other writings). This long process, that *via longissima* is also seen as the bulk of the work, to be followed by the *rubedo* (the reddening with new life), the *citrinitas* (yellowing) and finally the *cauda pavonis*, the achievement of the peacock's tail with the entire rainbow of colors which signify the end.

In our present series, the colors are not included. We have, instead, the austere, black and white presentation of the process, suitable for that equally austere yet life-filled process of *zazen*, of sitting and meditating. There are, indeed, series which are in color, but I am not familiar enough with them to contrast those with the original set. The same austerity and side-wise reference to sitting, *zazen*, is probably contained in the comment, "when a thought moves, another follows. . ." When we sit and focus upon our breathing, our emptiness, it is indeed the thoughts which come to disturb us, to push us away from our concentration. And it is our mind that we are trying to tame, that unruly free-associative mind which takes us away from that moment of true nothingness, in which there are no more thoughts, only the stillness, which brings Enlightenment.

How different is sitting, the *zazen*, and its aim, from our modern psychotherapy! Overcome the free-association, says our Zen-Master. Go with the free-association, says our Freudian analyst. Ignore the fantasies which arise, and let them go by, says the Buddhist teacher. Focus upon the fantasies and ultimately dialogue with them, says the Jungian analyst.

Does such instruction produce different results? It seems to. For the Freudian, we find the face just after we were born, the childhood desires and terrors which are father to the man. Our consciousness is to overcome these, to arrive at the maturity of full capacity to love and to work, to know the world and the psyche as it is without illusion. For the Buddhist, it is the face before we were born, and to discover our unity with nature, and our oneness with all life. For the Jungian, it is both of these, the link with collective, inner and outer, and the discovery of our Selves. So, the Jungian might be the intermediary between the two; the psychotherapy which aims at healing, love and work, and freeing from illusion, but at Enlightenment, too. This theme will occupy us once more at the end.

Let us consider, again, the words of Kaku-an, for the words, as we have said, continue with the consideration of the process and not, as the picture suggests, its conclusion.

Kaku-an tells us first that even the endless stream of associations "turns into truth" when Enlightenment prevails, but this is not the case when we are confused, uncentered, unknowing. So, it is not the content, he informs us, or its flow that deludes us but the place from which we relate to it. When we are centered, all is in harmony and understandable; when we are not, confusion makes it mere falsehood. Kaku-an is the great psychologist here. He is a combination behaviorist of the cognitive variety, a Jungian, and, of course, a Buddhist. Would that we could achieve now what he saw four hundred years ago!

He also tells us that we are oppressed not by the outside world, the objective world which we noted to be troublesome when we discussed the previous picture, but because of our own self-deceiving mind. Again it is our attitude, our center from which the confusion and trouble arises. These are hard words and wrong from an extraverted point-of-view (it is the social order, capitalism, communism, the environment, etc. which causes our problems), but right for the introvert. But Kaku-an is right all the same, at least when we are trying to deal with our own attitude, our own contribution to the oppression which falls upon us from without. If we can center, find the right relationship to it, then we are all right. The secret is that we can only find the right attitude to "it" and to "ourselves" when we include both, and just in the proportion that each "it" and "us" demands -- no more, no less. It is this, perhaps, that Kaku-an is referring to when he says, "Do not let the string loose, hold it tight, and allow no vacillation." I read this not only as an instruction in how to meditate efficiently, but a statement of the psychological condition: hold tight to the Self as it manifests, within and without; keep the event and the reaction in its particularity and do not let go until the resolution, the harmony, results. In either case, the advice is right, the medicine is strong, and hard to swallow.

This is the theme of the poem, as well, expressed more beautifully. Do not separate yourself from the Self, he advises, lest the animal wander away into defilement. When properly attended, the ox grows pure and docile, and finally -- and here, with more of an intuition than an achievement, as we saw in the first picture -- the animal, "without a chain, nothing binding, he will by himself follow the oxherd." What a promise this, and what a task: struggle and hold tight, relax and let go! No wonder we drive ourselves crazy in the search for Enlightenment and wholeness! But a hint is presented once more. The ox will come by himself when the time is right. He ultimately needs no chain, no discipline, only a relationship. And, though it is only hinted at and not expressed, we can guess that he will join us in this way because he wants to himself and not only because of our urgings and efforts. So, once more, Kaku-an holds out hope and direction.

Picture VI: Coming Home on the Ox's Back

> The struggle is over: the man is no more concerned with gain and loss. He hums a rustic tune of the woodman, he sings simple songs of the village boy. Saddling himself on the ox's back, his eyes are fixed on things not of the earth, earthy. Even if he is called, he will not turn his head; however enticed, he will no more be kept back.

> Riding on the animal, he leisurely wends his way home:

> Enveloped in the evening mist, how tunefully the flute vanishes away!

> Singing a ditty, beating time, his heart is filled with a joy indescribable!

> That he is now one of those who know, need it be told?

"The struggle is over, the *man* is no more concerned. . ." Now suddenly, we find that the boy has become a man. It is as if one is a youth when beginning the struggle with the instincts, and is a man when one has satisfactorily adjusted to them and to the world. That is certainly how it is in society and culture: the initiation into adulthood has indeed to do with the relation to our animal nature. But here the process of initiation is also made clear in the non-societal struggle in the spiritual world. Maturity of the soul requires an inner struggle with our animal nature as a way to Selfhood, and is concluded only when that is achieved. Is this true also for women? Is one a girl until one has related fully to the instinct? Maybe the imagery is different. Perhaps here the *Rosarium* pictures and their implied qualities of relationship and union is more germane. For girls to become women, in many societies, happens only with marriage. It is the *conjunctio* in the world which brings maturity. But then, again, perhaps it is not so different for women in the spiritual realm. The great individuation pictures illustrated in the *Villa of Mysteries*, and as described by Linda Fierz-David (1957) suggest that it is the self-same struggle with passion and the animal world which enables the woman of spirit to come to maturity of soul. So, perhaps these pictures of Zen transcend not only culture, East and West, but the male/female polarity as well. That is for women themselves to decide.

Here we can view the maturation of the spirit in its apparent finality: the struggle is over. The seeker is no longer concerned with gain and loss. What an achievement this is! When can any of us, in the West, transcend our endless striving for this and that, our bottomless pit of desire, our mad mind, which our host the American Indian finds as crazy? When do we find our heart, our earthy and rustic heart, our feeling for life and nature? Only when we do so are we grown up enough to sing the songs of the village boy, to feel free to express that youthful joy and optimism without being identified with it. Then are we simple, once more, and things are simple once again. The old Buddhist adage is here proved: in the beginning of the path to Enlightenment houses are houses, trees are trees; in the middle of the way, houses are no longer houses and trees are no longer trees; in the end, houses are once again houses and trees, trees. But they are simple again in a new way, redemption has occurred.

The man is saddled on the ox's back, he is firmly riding, feeling in contact with his instinctual life and that of the divine itself. His eyes are not fixed on earth however. He is free. He is free to follow heaven or earth. He is not just focussed on "gain and loss" as are the rest of us. Connected with the nature of the divine itself, he will no longer be enticed.

The poem tells us that he rides the animal and finds his way home. Is it not the animal itself which leads the way? This is the special wonder of this picture and these words. After all the struggle, the bridling and taming and disciplining of the animal, it is the ox itself which leads the way. The boy might say, "Look, Ma, no hands!" The man now rides the ox, but is led by him. He only plays his tuneful flute, he stays in touch with his feeling life and expresses it as best he can; direction is left to the Self, to the nature that he spent so much time relating to and taming.

Why are we so awed by this picture of "no hands?" Because we in the West have had a very different tradition of dealing with the animal, of coping with and expressing our animal natures. Think of our tradition of bull-fighting. True, it is a spectacle and a ritual, not a sport -- as some misguided souls see it. True also that the entire performance has the passion of self-discipline and relationship, just as we see here in the oxherding pictures. Most importantly true is the fact that the Matador and the bull are in such intimate relationship that at the final moment, when the bull is being killed, we know that deep secret shared only by the sincere participators therein: that man and animal are one, that Matador and bull share the same reality, that as the one kills the other, he also is killing/sacrificing himself. In this, therefore, and in the bullfight whose repeated presentation is the last great ritual having its roots in the Mediterranean past, we hear the echo of self-mastery and self-sacrifice, the virtues of the taming of Western passion. We may recall the religion of Mithraism, that great spiritual direction embraced by the Roman soldiers of antiquity and the nearly successful rival of Christianity in the early part of the aeon. Mithra, the hero, as Cumont tells us in *The Mysteries of Mithra*, (1956) sacrifices the bull of his own nature and carries a cornucopia of its riches upon his back. Deep and meaningful is this, but how different from the Zen portrayal! In our Western tradition *The King Must Die* (Renault, 1962) and the bull must die, but in the East, the bull lives, he guides us and is the basis of our being.

Perhaps this difference is an enlightening one for us all, in the East and West. Until the modern age, China and Japan turned within, sought perfection and differentiation in their own culture and time, valuing the taming of their own nature. We in the West, with our predatory birds (eagles) and our sacrificed gods and animals, turned our captured energy into conquest, victory over others and the world, and into subduing nature itself. Knowledge of the world is our achievement, not knowledge of the Self. World conversion is our success, not a transformation of Self. But, in the most modern day, all this, too, is over. There is a cry to end the bull-sacrifice in the West, an end to missionarizing, an end to conquest, and a turning toward Self-transformation. And, in the East, there is a dying of the tradition of Self-mastery and a turning to the outer achievements and "isms" of the West. They are even beginning to defeat the West at its own power game. So it is that a Westerner turns to oxherding pictures in awe and appreciation. Christianity may have failed to missionarize the world, but science has succeeded in doing so. Some say that Buddhism may be dying in the Orient, but it is alive and well in California and Europe. In the end, we learn from each other, and perhaps the synthesis is now building.

But let us return to the picture and the words. The heart of the man is filled with a joy indescribable and, if we look at the ox, do we not also see a smile, a head tilted upward, as if listening to the ditty being sung, the tune being played? The joy of the ox, in harmony with the man, is as great as the latter feels. In this is the true union, in this relationship is the reconciliation, the resolution of all our conflicts, all our disharmony. Would that we could know, as the seeker now knows.

Picture VII: The Ox Forgotten, Leaving the Man Alone

The dharmas are one and the ox is symbolic. When you know that what you need is not the snare or set net but the hare or fish, it is like gold separated from the dross, it is like the moon rising out of the clouds. The one ray of light serene and penetrating shines even before days of creation.

> Riding on the animal, he is at last back in his
> home
>
> Where lo! the ox is no more; the man alone
> sits serenely.
>
> Thought the red sun is high up in the sky, he
> is still quietly dreaming.
>
> Under a straw-thatched roof are his whip
> and rope idly lying.

The poem here both carries us onward, and links us back with picture VI, whereas poems of earlier pictures carried us beyond the image at hand. After the fulfillment of "coming home on the ox's back," the picture shows us where his true home is, atop the mountain. The mountain is a symbol of his aloneness, having achieved a "high-point" in his individuation/enlightenment. He has "attained," as the Hindus are fond of saying.

The poem tells us, "lo! the ox is no more." What does it mean that the ox is no more? Is he dead, vanished, or gone out of sight? None of these, since he is now integrated into the man, or transformed into the red sun or moon rising out of the clouds. The ox is "forgotten."

Kaku-an's words tell us that the ox is symbolic (and this known in the fifteenth century!) and that the dharmas (justice, law, practice) are one, namely unified. We thus learn that our struggle with instinct, with desire, with passion, with gain and loss was all a vehicle, a method, perhaps even a "snare" or "set net." All this was so real when we were struggling, but it is just illusion now, as we sit peacefully, contentedly, serenely upon the mountain top. We know, now, that theories, techniques, even images, are but vehicles and what we want is the "hare" or the "fish," the reality of the experience in its definiteness, concreteness. When we know this, it is gold from dross, alchemical transformation of the valued part from all the surround. East meets West in transformation and symbol.

Suzuki tells us that "picture VII completes the process of self-discipline; it marks the culmination of a struggle that has been going on even after the awakening of a new consciousness." Now we understand that "coming home" was not enough; "being home" was necessary.

Our man sits in meditation, even prayer, perhaps with his clasped hands before him, as he gazes up, at that "moon rising out of the clouds." What meditative joy in his reveries! What peace emerges in that mountain eyrie! His view is immense from that mountain, from that paper-thin walled cottage, in that deliciously sensitive oriental landscape. He sits alone, serenely. No more whip nor rope, no more discipline and effort and struggle. He has forgotten the ox, forgotten his struggle, forgotten even what he was searching for. Here it is.

But still, the red sun is high up in the sky, consciousness shines brightly around him. He is still quietly dreaming; he is still at one with the dream world, the inner world, as a friend, not a foe. The consciousness that now obtains is like the "one ray of light serene and penetrating"; it is the consciousness that was there always, "even before creation." He once more connects us with the Self-potential, the face before we were born, and we know it now as a Self-actual, as a presence. The Self is no longer projected on the ox, as we would say. Neither is there a need for the animal kind of awareness. This has its counterpart in the *Kundalini* picture series, (Avalon, 1958). In each of the lower chakra representations, there is an animal quality: an elephant, a kind of crocodile-devourer, a ram, a gazelle-like creature. Finally, at the level of the throat, the elephant which began at the muladhara (tail end first as happens also in the oxherding series), becomes transformed into a white elephant, and then at the forehead, where the one-eyed Ajna reins, there is no animal at all! I think it was Jung who somewhere remarked that this would mean that this level of consciousness does not require a bodily basis at all, it is psyche transcending. So it is here.

Sun and moon are also present, those polar twins of the alchemical series, and the mountain, too. Individuation continues. The process is not yet over.

Picture VIII: The Ox and Man Both Gone Out of Sight

> All confusion is set aside, and serenity alone prevails: even the idea of holiness does not obtain. He does not linger about where the Buddha is, and as to where there is no Buddha he speedily passes by. When there exists no form of dualism, even a thousand-eyed one fails to detect a loophole. A holiness before which birds offer flowers is but a farce.

> All is empty -- the whip, the rope, the man, and the ox:

> Who can ever survey the vastness of heaven?

> Over the furnace burning ablaze, not a flake of snow can fall:

> When this state of things obtains, manifest is the spirit of the ancient master.

What more might we in the West expect from such a process? In Picture VI, we found serenity and oneness with our animal nature and union with the longed-for God-head itself. In picture VII we went even beyond the wonder of instinct and found serenity and stillness. But now, "serenity alone prevails; even the idea of holiness does not obtain." A truly Eastern notion this: there is development beyond the holy, a condition in which there is no longer any worship nor seeking at all, not even after the divine! We no longer seek the Buddha, and quickly move away from where there is no Buddha. A true selflessness is to be found there, in our Western sense, where even desire for the divine is sacrificed.

Suzuki quotes for us in connection with this picture, a Western mystic, Meister Eckhart, in which the latter says (p. 202, 1964), "He alone hath true spiritual poverty who wills nothing, knows nothing, desires nothing." Even the desire to fulfill the will of God is an obstacle here. Now we understand the statement: "serenity alone prevails." When not even I am serene, then "serenity alone prevails." The ego is gone. Not only the ox, but now the man, too, has "gone out of sight."

It is this condition that Suzuki refers to when he states that a second awakening has taken place. What now obtains is absolute nothingness, symbolized by a empty circle. But this circle is not an ordinary one. It has no limits, because it is not circumscribed; it has no boundaries, and no actual center. Its center, really, is everywhere. At this point, we are informed, we enter ontology and find the mystery of the inward way (p. 200): "In spite of its eternally being empty (*sunya*), [it is] in possession of infinite values. It never exhausts itself." For us in the West, that definition is the mystic one of God. God is a circle whose center is everywhere and circumference nowhere, the mystic informs us. So here East and West meet, not in the definition of the divine, but in the experience of it. All numbers meet in the number beyond number: zero, the circle.

How are we to understand this from a psychological point of view? Jung was fond of commenting that the Eastern way of saying that the ego is totally obliterated made no sense to him. Who was it, he asked, that experienced this divine, if not the ego? If Jung seems to be right, how can we reply to the statement that when there is no form of dualism, no one, not even a thousand-eyed one, can find a loophole? There needs to be some observing consciousness, someone to report the experience, or else it does not happen. The resolution of this apparent paradox, it seems to me, comes from the poem itself.

"All is empty," says the poet, "the whip, the rope, the man and the ox." All partake of *sunya* emptiness, and none is more or less important than the other. All, in short, are part of a whole. This whole itself is nothing and everything, as is the *sunya* which is an ever-replenishing source and is also empty in itself. Without all the parts, the whole is nothing; without the whole, the part is nothing. Together, then, the part and whole are everything and nothing. Truly. Translated into psychological thought, we can say that the symbol of wholeness, the Self, is the mandala, the circle as here. This Self contains the ego, as well as the rest. There is, therefore, no distinction between Self and ego, between whole and part, and that here, at last, as Suzuki says, comes the "second awakening," where the relativization of the ego -- and the individual Self, too! -- occurs in such a way as to say that all are part of the larger and largest whole.

"Who can ever survey the vastness of heaven?" the poet says, and this the largest whole. Who, indeed, except heaven itself.

Psychologically, we would say that heaven, or the Self, is doing the surveying, and the ego is its vehicle. When there is no distinction between ego and Self, not even holiness occurs. That power of creativity of the blazing furnace melts any possibility of its dimming. And when the ego is truly in service of that wholeness, "manifest is the spirit of the ancient master." One might say that at this point the original spirit of the process of Enlightenment shows itself: ego and Self are one.

What is not shown in this picture, and what perhaps is the most difficult part of the process, is the way to the dethronement of that ego, that changing of the center of consciousness -- as Jung would say, from ego to Self. That process would entail another series of pictures with the ox now representing the ego, rather than the instincts. That battle is a much more crucial one for Westerners than Easterners, as Jung has shown us, since the Orient has tended, in the past, to hold a less distinct consciousness and to connect with the Self at the expense of the development of individuality -- at least in our Western sense. Kawai, the Japanese Jungian analyst (1981), has validated this understanding.

For us, in the West, we are continually taken over by one archetype after another when we undertake the journey, and often when we do not even start. Inflation is a natural consequence, Jung tells us (in the *Two Essays*, 1953) but it is our peculiar suffering all the same. Therefore, to come to this condition of wholeness, of the mandala in which ego and Self are one, is a great achievement indeed! Many may draw mandalas and copy gurus, but this activity, like the holiness before which birds offer flowers, is but a farce. The achievement requires a lifetime (lifetimes, in the Eastern sense.)

If we try to go deeper into this difference of East and West in the process of seeking Enlightenment, we can do no better than examine the vehicles. For the East, the method is meditation and the achievement of mindlessness, no content, nothingness. For the West, the method is prayer, or in psychotherapy, active imagination, the passion of relationship and union, as we have said before.

Going back one picture, to number VII, may give us a clue. The poem therein speaks of no longer needing the "snare" but the hare itself. One can look upon this from the methodological point of view and understand the snare or set-net as the technique of meditation itself. Once one has had the experience of Self, then meditation -- even the great and wonderful vehicle of the way -- is itself no longer necessary. When you have the animal, when you have the reality, then the method for achieving it is no longer needed.

It is at the point of the **experience**, as we have mentioned earlier, that East and West meet. Meditation is the Eastern way, and particularly the meditation of one-pointedness; whereas imagination is the Western way. Both lead to union, and when this is achieved, differences vanish. But the methods also include the goal: meditation with mind-lessness and ego-lessness on the way makes it easier for union at the end; imagination with consciousness and discrimination on the way makes union more difficult at the end.

The wonder is that what emerges is so much alike: clarity, serenity, joy, ego-lessness (in the sense of non ego-centric). Yet we know that Enlightenment, however vast, is always only partial when one remains in the mortal body. There is always a new ox to find and to tame, a new circle to come to. As long as we are alive, our wholeness is relative, and it is only for moments or periods where "not a flake of snow can fall." The *via longisima* is life-long. This means that the ego is always once more working, acting and being acted upon. The ox and man, though gone out of sight, generally come back in another process or path, brief or long. But once the process is undergone, one is never quite the same, the memory is always there. The "face before you were born," when experienced in this life, can always recall us, remind us, even when everything else is empty.

Picture IX: Returning to the Origin, Back to the Source

> From the very beginning, pure and immaculate, the man has never been affected by defilement. He watches the growth of things, while himself abiding in the immovable serenity of nonassertion. He does not identify himself with the maya-like transformations (that are going on about him), nor has he any use of himself (which is artificiality). The waters are blue, the mountains are green; sitting alone, he observes things undergoing changes.

> The return to the Origin, to be back at the Source -- already a false step this!

> Far better is it to stay at home, blind and deaf, and without much ado;

> Sitting in the hut, he takes no cognizance of things outside,

Behold the streams flowing -- whither nobody
knows; and the flowers vividly red -- for
whom are they?

How can one go beyond the mandala, the condition where ego and Self are one? Indeed, there are oxherding series, as we have seen (and as is shown in this book), where the process ends in just such a condtion; *sunyata* prevails, emptiness and fullness in the circle is the end of all. Yet Kaku-an, and not he alone, shows us that there is more to the process, that the condition of emptiness and even fullness, does not end the cycle.

What do we see in this next stage? An image of nature itself, a tree in its blossoming and its twisted trunk, almost racked. In it, however, are two more circles, now embedded in the very trunk of that tree. Could this be the sequel, intended or not? That Nature is beyond the abstraction of the circle? In any event, that is how I read this further stage in the development of the process. I see the fullness and life in the blossoms, the deadness and emptiness in the circles of the trunk. The opposites are once more united in the life of the tree.

This symbol of the *tree* is also one that transcends East and West. For us, in the West, there is, most importantly, the Tree of Life in our own main *sutra*, the Bible, reaching a differentiation and elaboration in the Jewish mysticism of the Kabbalah. That same Tree of Life was cut off from us, "in the beginning," when we fell out of paradise. A sword of fire separated us from it. But mysticism tells us that we can come once again to that tree when we discover, as Jesus also tells us in the later book, that "ye are Gods," that God and person are one. So, we have the techniques of the climbing of the Tree of Life, in Western mysticism and the occult (Regardie, 1969, 1984).

But the tree is also a world tree, and the tree of Hinduism, thus transcending East and West. That tree, with its roots going deeply into the earth and reaching up into heaven is a symbol for our own individuation as well. Heroes are born from it; gods die on it; we all live in it. So, perhaps, the tree is an even higher form than the circle. We reach that circle like the sun and moon themselves, paradoxically. We rise in consciousness, yet we fall onto the earth and into the play of life in that seamless whole of the tree. The tree has blossoms and dead wood, beauty and emptiness; it is a living symbol for wholeness.

This is not the view of Suzuki, however. Once again he thinks that we may get a distorted idea from the view of the tree as

Origin or Source. We might take it as another dualistic statement, with the man unattached and watching the maya-like transformations going around him. This might be true (p. 200, 1964) in *Sankhya* philosophy, "in which the *Purusha* quietly sits unmoved and unconcerned with the *Prakrit* going through an infinite series of antics." This is far from the case in Zen, Suzuki assures us. In a very beautiful and world-loving way, might I say, he asserts the value of action:

> **For the man will never be found "sitting in his hut." Not only does he take cognizance of things going on outside, but he is the things, he is the outside and the inside. Nor is he deaf and blind. He sees perfectly well even into the interior of an atom and explodes with it wherever it may fall regardless of its effects. But at the same time he sheds tears over human ignorance, over human follies and infirmities; he hastens to repair all the damages he produced, he contrives every possible method to prevent the recurrence. He is forever kept busy doing this, undoing that.**

What a heartfelt commitment to human action! What a profound realization that even the Enlightened one is endlessly making blunders, causing damage, and must spend half of his time repairing the evil he has done personally, as well as mourning and having compassion for human folly. One thinks of when and where Suzuki said these words. It was in the Switzerland of 1954, not so long after the terrible events at Hiroshima and Nagasaki. Could not this have been in the back of his mind when he spoke of not being deaf and blind, and seeing perfectly well "even into the interior of an atom"? I think that Suzuki was quite aware of the paradox of human good and evil, in a very personal way, when he added that with the explosion of this atom, that the Enlightened man "explodes with it wherever it may fall regardless of its effects." That he can rise above this experience of evil done to his people, yet not be blind to mankind's follies on all sides is great enough. To take on his own charge of repairing the damage he has himself done puts him into a deep brotherly relationship with the best that the West has to offer. Jung, particulary in his profound vision of the evil in the divine situation and man's place in it (e.g. *Answer to Job* Vol, 11 1952), is similarly grasped and made aware.

But perhaps Suzuki's passion is really less connected with this picture, despite its stillness and the non-assertion recommended by the remarks. It seems as if his words are more relevant to picture X. Indeed, at the end of his passionate statement, Suzuki says that the Enlightened one is "forever kept busy doing this, undoing that," and that this is just what "daubed with mud and ashes" means. This "daubedness" belongs to Picture X, to which we shall turn shortly. First, however, we should look more kindly at the words of Kaku-an in this picture.

Kaku-an tells us that the man has never been affected by defilement, from the very beginning. Here we learn that even the process itself may be an illusion. We were never out of harmony at all, we never left "home." Not only is it better to be blind and deaf, and to stay home and not complain and not have the audacity to start on the path to Enlightenment, but even if we think so, we have never even left. It is a false step, an illusion to even think so. What then, does this mean? Have we not struggled with the sutras, found the ox, disciplined him, given him up, sacrificed our ego, done all those wonderful and terrible things that have shown us the truth?

Apparently not. The waters are blue, the mountains are green. "Things undergo change." Maybe that is the point: changes are just happening, even those we think that we are accomplishing. Even those changes and efforts perhaps are an illusion of ours: we think that we are doing them, accomplishing them, but it is Nature itself that is doing them. It is Nature, here shown in the wonderful tree, that is expressing itself and we are foolish to think that we did it, to chalk up to ourselves such special achievement, ego-centric or not. The poet hints that the whole process is one of Nature itself. Does not this strike at the same wisdom that alchemy tells us when it says that it is nature that battles nature, it is nature that overcomes nature? Are we not part of that *natural* process of life finding itself, becoming conscious of itself? So that beyond the abstraction of the circle and its fulness and emptiness, a circle which is not found in nature, is the reality of Nature itself, in which that process manifests. In Picture VIII we are told that in the circle, "manifest is the spirit of the ancient master." In Picture IX, perhaps, we can say "manifest is the spirit of nature, Herself."

In this, I would think, is the recognition of the feminine principle at a deeper level, an appreciation of which must be fully apprehended before this process is completed. The circle, indeed, is a feminine symbol, showing wholeness at an abstract level; the tree brings us into Nature Herself in all Her complexity, and the seeker must stay here, in his inwardness until he/she knows this.

> Sitting in the hut, he takes no cognizance of
> things outside,

Behold the streams flowing -- whither nobody
knows; and the flowers vividly red -- for
whom are they?

I would venture to say that he remains sitting and inward until
he can behold the streams and the red flowers, without knowing
for whom or where they go. In so doing, he sees that Nature -- and
he as a part of Nature -- has its own Being and aims that he can not
fathom. In this day before the creation of the theory of evolution,
he can grasp the wonder of nature, in himself and in life, and find
that he can not be other than himself, that from the beginning and
in the middle and in the end, he is himself within the totality of
existence. It is Nature who is expressing Herself. And that is the
answer to the koan, for whom are the flowers vividly red? It is for
Nature Herself.

One thing remains to be addressed in this picture. It is the
puzzling statement which follows the understandable, "He does
not identify himself with the maya-like transformations (that are
going on around him). . ." After this comes, "nor has he any use of
himself (which is artificiality)." What does this mean, to have no
use of one's self? Is it a repeat of the notion that the ego itself is
valueless, just a part, like all other parts of the whole? Or is
something else intended?

A possible answer may be found in the Zen story of the tree
which remained in a forest when all others were cut down. When
this tree was queried as to how it was able to survive when the rest
were cut down, it replied that it "had no use for itself." All the
other trees were beautiful, had good wood in them, were needed
for houses, etc., but this tree was neither beautiful nor valuable. It
was "unworthy" the tale says. It was of no value to anyone, no
threat to anyone, unworthy, and so it survived. The deeper
meaning we can guess was that it was of value only to itself. Thus
does this tree coincide perhaps with the tree of our picture, it is
worthy only to itself. So does the man have no use of himself. Is he
of value only to himself?

This reminds one of the statement, "What others think of me is
none of my business," -- another variation of this paradox of being
of no use and full of value at the same time. Such truths are
relative to time and person: balm or poison, depending upon the
moment.

That such a paradox can be true in the transpersonal dimension,
larger than that of the personal existence, is suggested, once
more, by the fact that it is a tree here that is portrayed at the

highest level, higher even than the circle. The whole transpersonal character of the transformation process is thereby portrayed, just as it is in the *Rosarium* pictures, where the entire series begins with symbols of nature -- sun, moon, snake, etc. -- along with a well or fountain. Somewhere we learn through these two portrayals of the Enlightenment/Individuation process that it is not for ourselves ("no use") but for nature (God), that we undertake it. The paradox unravelled, of course, is that when we are a conscious part of this wholeness, sharing that work of transformation, we are blessed.

When East and West meet in this experience, therefore, we can understand even the highest paradox of all: God and no-God, is true.

Picture X: Entering the City with Bliss-Bestowing Hands

His thatched cottage gate is closed, and even the wisest know him not. No glimpses of his inner life are to be caught; for he goes on his own way without following the steps of the ancient sages.
Carrying a gourd he goes out into the market, leaning against a staff he comes home. He is found in company with winebibbers and butchers, he and they are all converted into Buddhas.

Bare-chested and barefooted, he comes out
   into the market place;

Daubed with mud and ashes, how broadly he
   smiles!

There is no need for the miraculous power
   of the gods,

For he touches, and lo! the dead trees are
   in full bloom.

We come now, as Suzuki says (p. 201, 1964), to "the final stage of the drama." For Suzuki, the final stage is that the cottage is not only shut, but cottage and gate are gone. No one can locate where the Enlightened one is. "Yet he is ubiquitous; he is seen in the market place, he is seen on farms, he is seen with the children, with men and women, he is seen with the birds and animals, among the rocks and mountains. Anything he touches grows into full bloom, even the dead are awakened."

In short, the final stage of the drama for Suzuki is one in which the Enlightened one returns to the world and ordinary man, but has bliss-bestowing hands. He contrasts this bare-chested and barefooted figure of our picture with that of Christ in the Last Judgment painted by Michelangelo in the Sistine Chapel. The latter, says Suzuki, is almost impossible to approach, much less touch, for he is majestically and vigorously passing out judgments. "If you come near him, you would surely be torn to pieces and thrown into eternal fire." This is not the case with the Bodhisattva, in Picture X, who is so genial. What a difference, it seems, in the two images of the Enlightened One in the world! Perhaps Suzuki does not understand (or understands too well!) our Western struggle with duality, since that same Christ, full of judgment in the Apocalypse of John (like his Father in the Old Testament!), is also the Lamb. We, too, have our variety of images of Enlightenment and service of the Holy One. And we can understand very well this Easterner contrasting the Zen image of the Enlightened figure with our Western version, in which our version comes out rather second-best.

The difference, perhaps, is in the degree and quality of humanity which emerges. Our usual Western image of the God-Man may be all too kind, redemptive, and far from ordinary man. He is not subject to the the passions that plague us. He longs to be with the ordinary man, but one has the feeling that even though he seeks the company of "winebibers and butchers" he is unlikely to get drunk or enjoy women in a carnal way. The center of the Eastern Enlightened one, as Suzuki tells us, is in the belly, he is a belly-man. Our Jesus, on the other hand, centers in the heart; He is a God-man of love. Belly-centerdness is quite instinctive, as Suzuki tells us, and grounds itself in the earth, in life. Our Christ-consciousness, on the other hand, as manifested in Jesus and in love, is in life, but looks toward heaven, toward the transcendence of life and death. Both images have "bliss-bestowing," healing hands, but our Zen figure is almost fat, whereas Christ is usually portrayed as lean, even gaunt. No cross of the suffering of the opposites prevails in the Enlightened one -- the *sine qua non* of the God-man. Instead he carries a big cornucopia on his back, an unending source of bliss. Does this carrying of the cornucopia hearken back to the Mithra figure of Western antiquity, who also carried the sacrificed bull upon his back, equally laden with riches? This may be the brother of our Christ figure, who remained more with the symbol of conflict and resolution, and thus has less of Eastern wholeness than he might. After all, He must unite being God and Man, whereas our Zen hero, has "no need for the miraculous power of the gods," nor, we might add, is he a god, either!

Other differences are apparent in the carrying of the gourd, a symbol of *sunyata*, emptiness. Yet Suzuki quotes the great Christian Mystic, Meister Eckhart, in saying (p. 202, 1964):

> A man shall become truly poor and as free from his creature will as he was when he was born. And I say unto you, by the eternal truth, that as long as ye desire to fulfill the will of God, and have any desire after eternity and God, so long are ye not truly poor. He alone hath true spiritual poverty who wills nothing, knows nothing, desires nothing.

Eckhart's Enlightened man is close to the Zen man in this. The figure here carries only a staff which, according to Suzuki, indicates that he carries no extra property at all, for he "knows that the desire to possess is the curse of human life." So, our two figures are alike, yet different, as like and different as the experience of East and West.

From the psychological point-of-view, we see two ways of viewing and experiencing the Self. In the West we have much to learn from this Eastern representation. When we are with our smallness, we can see ourselves serving the Self-within as our larger totality, like Christ, the God-within. When we are with our "bigness" (or "smallness" in another way) we can see ourselves in the undivided totality of the Buddha-man here represented. Luckily, we need not choose, only experience.

Let us look a bit more at other aspects of this tenth picture. We note, first all, that the figure shown here is no longer the youth of the early pictures. Neither is he the "man" who looked the same but was transformed into spiritual manhood by picture VI. We now see an old man, and realize that this ten-picture process is a life-time path, not a single event. To finally arrive at this destination (and we should not even have started out or thought to leave, as we are reminded in Picture IX), apparently requires not only meditation, study, and life-experience, but also just takes a long time! This surely can be attested to by the poor souls (all of us), East and West, who have been on that path for lifetimes!

Why should it take so long?·It just does, one is inclined to answer, in a Zen way, perhaps. But another answer comes from the realization that the resolution of such profound opposites entails work not only in the complex nature of the human being, but, as we have said before, in the paradoxical nature of the divine principle itself. It is this principle -- as we experience it in image, thought and deed -- that is going through evolution and slow change. As if to underline this fact, our final picture once more gives us the symbol of the tree, as it did in Picture IX. Now the tree frames the Enlightened one, and its blossoms go forward to the other person in the picture, the young man.

Much can be made about this new appearance. All through these pictures there has been either one boy or man, or no-one. Now we suddenly find two figures, the Enlightened one of age, and this youth meeting him in pleasure and joy. Is it not close to the truth to conjecture that this young man is another version of our original seeker, as he looked in the first picture? And that a function of our Enlightened one is, indeed, to help just such creatures as he was in the beginning to advance on their way? So it seems to me. The student becomes Master, and instructs new students. Thus is the process carried onwards.

The Tree of Life covers both seeker and teacher, and the long path is like nature itself, slowly growing with concentric rings of development, showing hardness and softness, resistance and flexibility, sweet-smellingness and decay. Both seekers, master and student, carry emblems of that same Tree: the one his staff of chosen poverty of spirit; the other his ordinary staff carrying his few possessions, symbol of his actual poverty in the same area. A happy meeting and a happy union. "He and they are all converted into Buddhas."

It remains for us to contrast this last picture of the ten with the last picture of Jung's *Rosarium* series. In the latter, there is a hermaphroditic figure who represents the union of King of Queen, a single figure combining all that has been achieved. In the beginning was only the vessel, the bath, the well. All through the middle there was the pair of King and Queen, opening, uniting, struggling, dying. At the end, there is the Empress, the union of male and female, with the accent on the feminine. In the oxherding series we began with a person. This person was joined by the animal, in which there was struggle and resolution. Then the animal was gone, the person was gone, nature remained. At the end there is achievement (the Enlightened one), and relationship (the student, the others). It seems to me that again we discover the contrast of the methods, East and West. In the East, aloneness is the way, meditation the method, and, in the end, relationship with others. In the West, the vessel is relationship itself and the capacity to stand alone is the achievement. There is a useful complementarity of the two, it seems to me. The same aloneness, however, ultimately adheres to both. "He goes on his way without following the steps of the ancient sages," is said of our Master, and so can it be said of the Western Master. Easy to proclaim, hard to attain or deserve.

All the same, when the "end" comes, the "dead trees are in full bloom," and we experience the "bliss-bestowing hands" of such a person, such a moment, such a relationship. What is not stated here, but is said by Suzuki in the last picture, as we noted, is that the Enlightened one still does damage and still tries to repair the damage that has been done, his own or that of others. "He is forever kept busy doing this, undoing that." So, then, we are in the right company when we are with winebibbers and butchers, for such are we, too.

Epilogue

What remains to be said after this all-too-brief yet "noisy" Western peregrination through the oxherding series? First of all, what wants to be said is a statement of thanks to Kaku-an and to Suzuki for their enormous gifts to us in the West of these enchanted pictures, poems and commentaries. In these days of psychic disintegration and breakdown of society, we are deeply indebted to those ancient representations of Eastern wisdom which can illuminate our individual paths and give us solace to know that many of our problems in such a quest were already seen and known in different climes, cultures and religions. The unique clarity of Kaku-an's words and pictures are especially Enlightening. We have seen, more than once, how this series complements the understanding of individuation as portrayed in the *Rosarium* series, interpreted by Jung. The two series together high-light the wisdom of the one against the other and bring into relief what each culture or way has achieved. The two are truly complementary and one hopes that this comparison contributes to the further marriage between the spirits of East and West.

Secondly, the very portrayal of the individuation process in both sets has perforce cast some reflection on the surrounding society and cultural spirit. The question arises as to what this individuation process means for the culture itself. Jung, in the epilogue to his discussion of the transference in the *Rosarium* series, says: (par. 539, 1946):

> The symbols of the circle and the quaternity, the hallmarks of the individuation process, point back, on the one hand, to the original and primitive order of human society, and forward on the other to an inner order of the psyche. It is as though the psyche were the indispensable instrument in the reorganization

of a civilized community as opposed to the collectivities which are so much in favour today, with their aggregations of half-baked mass-men. This type of organization has a meaning only if the human material it purports to organize is good for something. But the mass-man is good for nothing -- he is a mere particle that has forgotten what it is to be human and has lost its soul. What our world lacks is the *psychic connection*; and no clique, no community of interests, no political party, and no State will ever be able to replace this. It is therefore small wonder that it was the doctors and not the sociologists who were the first to feel more clearly than anybody else the true needs of man, for, as psychotherapists, they have the most direct dealings with the sufferings of the soul.

Since Jung's day, a quarter of a century and more ago, the cultural breakdown has continued and the "isms" and cliques have increased. There is no indication that his hope for a community based on the psychic connection has gained ground either. As I have pointed out elsewhere (Spiegelman 1984), there is no apparent increase in connectedness among religious communities or even psychological communities, for that matter. Jungian societies and clubs, for example, are no more "soul" communities than any of our traditional groups and societies, and suffer the same back-biting, gossip, power-struggles, etc. that we are accustomed to in other groups.

Jung's hope was for the individual dealing with his own soul, withdrawing the projection of his shadow, and seeing to his own integration and wholeness. Both of our picture-series show us how this is done and also show that society is, perforce, involved. The oxherding series ends in a return to society and a full participation in ordinary life. The Rosarium pictures not only suggest that the individuation process requires partners (the couple), but Jung asserts that this process is not even possible without it (par. 445 ff, 1946). Kinship libido, (the necessity for close ties), and endogamous union (the need to integrate the opposites spiritually and internally), are of equal importance, says Jung, and neither can happen without the other.

Our pictures, though, show the Western individual being whole and alone, while our Eastern series show a return to society. Eastern society, perhaps, has experienced slightly less disintegration than the West, if we use crime rates, wars, expansionism, revolution and the like as measures, but they are not very far behind us. Are we to conclude that only the continual work of the individual on himself is of value, as some Jungians aver? The fact that projection continues so forcefully among Jungians suggests that the unconscious is "trying" indeed to separate people, as well as connect them, so that the evidence would favor that hypothesis: we are compelled to differentiate by the thrust of the unconscious itself, which makes for separation, through misunderstanding, and through the process of enemy-formation. We would not be ready, then, from the apparent evidence, for this newer society or group with "soul-connection."

My own experience would tend to agree with the previous formulation, however painful it seems. Not only ongoing groups and societies, but even those formed with the express intention of building the "new world" of psychological understanding or soul-connection routinely fail. I would think, then, that it is probably too soon to even speculate about that society of the future in which soul-connection would have primacy, along with the value of individuation and Enlightenment as a path. All that we can do is tend to our own process, which, perforce, thrusts us back into life, as Suzuki so beautifully expresses. I would add, however, that nature, with its deep and powerful instinct of kinship-libido, will not stand still for this continual disintegration and that She will experiment with us all, in the form of group-conflicts, and in the construction of new situations. Else what is the meaning of picture number X of the oxherding series and number 1 of the *Rosarium* series?

As I write these lines, I sit in Los Angeles in the Summer of 1984 and note that the Olympic Games. held in this city, seem to be just such an experimental ground. The upsurge of joy and patriotism experienced by many millions accross this country as the flaming torch was carried from state to state and passed from hand to hand, startled almost everyone. No such feeling for this country had been expressed since World War II. Yet this patriotism is in connection with a non-warlike event in which nations of the world participate and both individual excellence and group pride are at stake. I think that this event is just such a living symbol of what the psyche may be trying to produce. By this I mean that the psyche is trying to form a world-community, which many have realized for a long time, and which was visually seen in the "planet earth" experience when the first astronauts landed on the moon. This world-community, apparently, is both a whole (of nations) and separate (glorification of difference, of separation of cultures). But it also values supremely the performance of the individual, going beyond all nations, states and groupings. It is a union via the flesh, (sport), at this point, and successful, despite the politicization and the withdrawal of nations over the last few Olympics. Yet those who withdraw suffer, not the participants, and even terrorism can not kill the event. The arts, too, are included, in the cultural Olympics and destined, I believe, to have an even greater role in future celebrations.

It is striking to me that conscious political attempts at unity, e.g. the United Nations, should be corrupted and almost defeated -- as was the League of Nations -- by parochialism, selfishness and narrow-mindedness, whereas the Olympics, begun earlier and resuming an ancient ritual, should both grow and gain in stature. It is tending to produce world-brotherhood/sisterhood itself, as we can see from the increased participation of all races and both sexes.

So there is at least some evidence of the psyche's attempt at producing social structures in which both the individual and the group are valued. **But the Olympics is no fosterer of consciousness nor Enlightenment, and we must remain quite alone in that quest, just as the Masters of East and West have told us**. We take solace in our process, however, and find our kinship libido where it occurs, as an unexpected and valued meeting of individuals, both in the concrete world and in the world of the spirit where the *inner* temple, church, and synagogue reign, and where the *Rosarium* and the Oxherding Pictures have both their origin and their goal.

REFERENCES

Avalon, Arthur, *The Serpent Power*, Ganesh & Co., Madras, 1958 (original edition, 1918), 508 pp. plus approx. 100 Sanskrit pp).

Cumont, Franz, *The Mysteries of Mithra*, Dover, New York, 1956 (original French edition 1902), 239 pp.

Doran, Robert M., S.J. Jungian Psychology and Christian Spirituality (in three parts) *Review for Religious*, Vol. 38, 1979/ pp. 497-510; Vol. 5, pp. 742-752; Vol. 6 pp. 857-866.

Fierz, Linda, *Psychological Reflections on the Fresco Series of the Villa of the Mysteries in Pompeii*, Kristine Mann Library, A.P.C. of New York, 1957, 190 pp.

von Franz, Marie-Louise, *Introduction to the Intepretation of Fairy Tales*, Spring Publications, 1970. 155 pp.

Jung, C.G. *Two Essays on Analytical Psychology*, Collected Works Vol. 7, 1953. Original 1918 & sequel editions.

Jung, C.G. *Psychology of the Transference*, in Collected Works, Vol. 16. Original, 1946.

Jung, C.G. *Answer to Job*, in Collected Works, Vol. 11. Original, 1943.

Jung, C.G. *Mysterium Conjunctionis*. Vol. 14. Original 1954.

Kawai, Hayao. "Violence in the Home." *Japan Quarterly.* Vol. XXIII, No. 3, July-September 1981, pp. 370-377

Miyuki, Mokusen. Various articles, *passim*, in this book. 1985.

Regardie, Israel. *The Complete Golden Dawn System of Magic.* Falcon Press. 1104 pp. Phoenix Az. 1984.

Regardie, Israel. *The Tree of Life.* Samuel Weiser, Inc., NY. 1969. Original 1932. 285 pp.

Renault, Mary. *The King Must Die.* Pantheon Books, New York, 1962.

Standard Dictionary of Folklore, edited by Maria Leach. 2 vols. Funk and Wagnall, New York, 1949, 1196 pp.

Spiegelman, J. Marvin. *The Tree: Tales in Psycho-mythology.* Falcon Press. Phoenix Az. 1982. Original 1975. 464 pp.

Spiegelman, J. Marvin. *The Quest.* Falcon Press. Phoenix Az. 1984. 175 pp.

Spiegelman, J. Marvin. *The Love.* To be published.

Spiegelman, J. Marvin. "Psychotherapy and the Clergy: Fifty Years Later." *Journal of Religion and Health,* 1984, Vol. 23, No.1, pp. 19-32.

Suzuki, D.T. *Manual of Zen Buddhism.* Grove Press, New York, 1960. Original 1935. 192 pp.

Suzuki, D.T. "Awakening of a New Consciousness in Zen," in *Man and Transformation,* Papers from Eranos, edited by Joseph Campbell, Vol 5, Routledge and Kegan Paul, London, 1964. Original 1954.

White, Victor. *God and the Unconscious.* World Pub. Co., New York, 1961. Original 1952. 287 pp.

THE RONIN
A Fictional Portrayal Of
The Oxherding Pictures
By J. Marvin Spiegelman

PREFATORY NOTE

The Ronin, at times addresses himself to the Knight and the Arab, whom he discovers at the end of his journey, at the Tree of Life. In this book, it is not essential to know their tales, but for those who are interested see, *The Tree: Tales in Psycho-Mythology* (Falcon Press, 1982).

I

I am a Ronin -- or rather, I have been a Ronin, and am no more. A Ronin, my friends, in our language, is a warrior, a samurai who has no lord. He wanders in search -- because a man without a master, a warrior without a lord, a disciple without a guru, what is he? Do not answer, for you two men, Sir Knight and Sir Arab, already know what I mean. I can tell this by your stories, although I am puzzled by much of what you say.

I only know that I am here with you now, in that place that is called Eden for you, Sir Knight, and Paradaizo for you, Sir Arab, and that, in truth it is the same for me -- although we call it "The Pure Land." It is indeed a miracle for us all to be here, as you would call it, Sir Knight. I am loathe to call it that myself because the miraculous has no special place in my view. There is no need for such a word since all life is miraculous.

My view on the matter is expressed by one of our Masters, who said, "I do not rely on God; I respect Him." You can see at once, Sir Knight and Sir Arab, how we differ.

We have come together for a purpose, it seems. We have come here to understand one another and to embrace one another. This we can do only after we have told our stories. I am desirous of telling you my tale, but first I must tell you, Sir Knight, and you, Sir Arab, some of my reactions to your stories. You, Sir Arab, have already done this for the Knight, with your first two parables, which I find most interesting. Thus I must tell you my own reactions, and then get on with my own tale.

Compared with my experiences, Sir Knight, yours seem more complex, with emotions and divisions which seem different from my own. For me, there is only one triangle, not two. My experience of myself consists of my "self" with all its faults and sufferings, the saving force of the Buddha, and finally, the experience or the reality of the Wordless realm: Emptiness Sunyata, Suchness, Naturalness; whatever the word. Just one little triangle.

I have a difficult time feeling such symbols as God, Goddesses, Angels, Snakes. I understand bits and parts which parallel Buddhistic thoughts. Such as the idea of the incompleteness of God without man. Amida's Vow, for example. He chose never to seek absolute perfection while even one sentient being suffered. Or Amida, too, as a parent (because of its emotional meaning, not metaphysical), and human beings, his children. But Amida can't be a parent without children.

Most of all, the union of opposites is a central idea in Buddhism. Actually, it is the only important idea. There are numerous opposites which are stated as: This world is, as is, the Pure Land. The world of Birth, Suffering, and Death is, as is, Nirvana. Defilement and Ignorance is, as is, the Supreme Understanding. Man and the Absolute Truth are, as is, One.

In your story, Sir Knight, from the Buddhist standpoint, the snake, the witch, the goddess, the horse, the forest, the God, the ocean, the maiden, the flashes of light, and even you, Oh Knight, are all One.

For you, Sir Arab, I have only compassion. Your way seems simpler and more direct to me. Maybe you are more Oriental, like myself. I too have had to deal with the animals, as you will see, though our solutions are different.

Gentlemen, it is strange. I feel close to you both because our goal is the same and the intensity of our drive is the same. But I feel different because you want to know and experience all the parts and thus bring them into union, while I go from the standpoint of denying everything, even the denial itself.

You know, I really have nothing to say. Life is like a sword, glinting in the sun. As simple as that, there is nothing to say. And we live on the edge of that sword; one slip and one meets death. To be able to die without fear is all that matters. Until then, just drink your *sake* and do what you must. Wander the earth, like a lion. Like a lion, die when your time comes, leaving no trace. For a man who had nothing to say, I've said quite a bit! Perhaps I have something in common with my Western friends, after all. Ha!

Now, to my own story.

As I have said at the outset, I have been a Ronin, a warrior without a Lord. It was not always so. When I was a youth, I apprenticed myself to a school of swordsmanship. We were many, we students, and we served our Lord and teacher devotedly. I was a reserved type, and accustomed to staying by myself. I was inclined to be cold and distant, even though my burning heart was filled with desire and emotion. It is often so with us, a fact which Westerners are not able to grasp very well.

I trained long and diligently. I struggled so hard, in fact, that I was often exhausted and in despair at my inability to reach my goal and master my task. In time, however, I grew very proficient -- so proficient, indeed, that I was able to defeat all my fellow pupils. At length, my Master acknowledged that he had nothing more to teach me. He blessed me and told me to go forth for further enlightenment. I bowed and went forth in joy and anticipation. I traveled throughout the land and sought encounters with swordsmen of every shape and talent. Sometimes I was defeated and sometimes I was victorious and with every encounter my skill grew. I was able, in time, to find other Masters who took me further in my craft. After many years of effort, I was able to perfect myself to a degree which seemed satisfactory.

It came to pass, however, that when I returned to my ancestral home, I was honored, but deceived. My skill and talent were beyond question, but my former Masters grew old and narrow. They were jealous, it seemed, of what I had accomplished and were in fear of losing their power. As it is, sometimes, with the old who cannot bend gracefully, they turned ever more rigid. I sorrowed, for it is in the nature of my land to respect the old and do everything possible to avoid the shame of losing face. I tried to keep my peace and do what I could to advance our common school of swordsmanship. In time, pupils sought me out as a Master. They went not to the Elders, and it was for this, I think, that the Old Ones grew even more jealous and irritated. Gossip increased, and I know not what was said of me.

When the time came for me to be fully acknowledged as a Master in my own right, the Elders banded together and looked piously down their noses at me. They nodded their hoary heads and said that I was not ready, that I was more a butcher than a swordsman, and so on. At first, I could not believe my ears, and I laughed. When I saw that they meant what they said, I became both furious and disconsolate. What could I do? Thy refused to reason or discuss. They looked for my submission, without even being honest enough to openly demand it. They hid in their pomposity, for they were, no doubt, afraid of my swordsmanship.

There was nothing to do except leave the Masters and the School and wander alone in the world. A Ronin. A warrior without a Lord. A disciple without a Master. A Master without recognition.

I wandered for a long time. After a year or so, I was no longer furious at the deception and betrayal by my former teachers, and was able to realize that what they said had a grain of truth in it. I was Master of my craft, but not Master of myself. I was, indeed, still attached to fame, recognition, power -- in short, to desire. I knew full well that the swordsman's craft was nothing without Enlightenment, and that I was, in truth, immersed in the illusion of this world -- bound up with ignorance and desire.

I resolved to retreat into the forest, where I could meet myself alone, without a Master, without assistance, and without a light.

II

I retreated into the forest where I remained alone for many days and nights. At first, I could think of nothing but my own despair. I was alone and lonely. This was a shock to a man like myself, who had been very used to thinking of himself as a lone one, who can wander the world without need of anyone. Ha! I thought, this is salutary in itself -- I must have been attached to the idea that I am alone and a lone one. My secret desire for fame and recognition is no better and no worse than this secret illusion that I can be utterly non-attached to people.

So, I accepted my loneliness and despair and came running back to my friends. I acknowledged all this without losing face and thus could return to my isolation and aloneness in a new way. I understood that one needed one's aloneness and isolation, along with one's need for family and friends. My mountain retreat was no place, but a state of mind, and a condition to which I could go at any time.

With this, I decided to look at the state of my soul. It was clearly an animal, a kind of ox or bull. I was well aware that my main preoccupation over many years had been to somehow cope with that animal inside me which was black as black can be, and wild and unruly and given to fits and starts and wanderings of all sorts. That animai of my wildly ignorant and lustful soul! Every desire that I have ever known was contained therein. Even the desire not to desire was contained in the hairy beast of that wild and snorting creature. Yes, I had seen him in every state: asleep, lusting, chaotic, well-ordered and disciplined, wild and adventuresome, frightened, joyous and aggressive. I did everything possible to tame him. I restrained him with ropes. I whipped him with as many lashes as I could manage. Yes, I had done all these things. I had even given him his full way. To which he responded with whims and chaos and hungers which immediately set the rest of my soul into guilt and despair all over again.

I was no stranger to the animal of my soul and all his movements. So this time it was no small surprise to see that he had whitened considerably! That was extraordinary! After all these years of taming and fighting and struggling with this passionate bull of my soul, with all his rages, lusts, disregardings -- now I saw him, indeed, whitening, whitening, whitening. How was this possible?

Now, I had to reflect. All these years of my effort and now when I simply accepted my needs to be with people, and accepted my needs to be alone, as well, now my poor bull was whitening. I could only conclude that he had whitened because I had accepted him! But I had also to conclude that I could accept him because he had whitened. Yes, a *koan*, indeed. The sound of one hand clapping. It is the same. The bull whitens because you accept him, and you accept him because he has whitened. So that is what those old foolish Masters were always talking about? Well, so be it. I will not challenge it; here in front of my nose is a whitening Bull! Indeed, I shall have to see how it is that he whitens. Will he wander off again? Shall I follow him? Shall I let him go? Should I discipline him?

Oh, there is despair! All the rights and wrongs, all the shoulds and shouldn'ts. Then my bull is black again, and one must start from the beginning. How will I ever learn that what is, is what matters. How will I learn to accept that I cannot accept? Oh, oh! There he goes, down and around and biting his own tail, and I whip him and defeat him, and he laughs and is morose, and I am a fool once more! Ha!

Now I simply stay with him. There he is, white and black, with the rope tied into his nostrils, but the rope hangs loosely. He looks at me; I look at he. He smiles, I smile. I go sit upon his back. Will he accept me? I sit, comfortably. Then he senses my anxiety, and he throws me. I am back on the ground, and he laughs. I laugh as well, but I beat him again. He groans, and I laugh. He laughs and I groan.

He is not yet ready. I am not yet ready. I cannot sit upon his back, but I can walk with him, and by his side. This I can do.

So, we walked together for many days. I held the reins very loosely -- so loosely at times that it was as if I did not hold them at all. Often I would look at him to see how he was. Now, when I smiled, he smiled back. That in itself told me that he was a most remarkable bull-ox. A smiling bull-ox? Yes, that, too, is like the sound of one hand clapping, or where your lap goes when you stand up.

I rejoiced: the Smile of the Bull-Ox! Now I laughed. I laughed and laughed and laughed. Everything was becoming very amusing to me. Was I going mad? No, surely not. The cosmos was a very great joke: It was the sound of a Bull-ox smiling.

Now I could sit and play my flute. I played at first carefully and delicately. I did not want to stir up this smiling bull-ox. But no, had I forgotten? Music can charm the beast, and so it could, and so it did. I played sad songs and mournful ones, and I wept. I played happy songs and I laughed. Then I sang. I sang every song I knew, and many that I did not know, but simply made up. My voice was first parched and squeaky, and too loud and too soft. It needed an oiling, or a tempering, just the way that my sword did. I tempered it, with sweet water and wine, did I temper it. Heated rice-wine, how softly it goes down the gullet! How delicate it is! How little it affects you! Until you stand up and are required to sit right down again.

But such a fuss about my needs! That is too demeaning of the swordsman! With that, the bull turned black again, and snorted and ran about, and kicked me and made me very nervous indeed.

You know of such bull-oxes in the West, do you not? Yes, of course you do. I had forgotten. You, Sir Knight, surely know of that tradition of the vaulting of the beast, and you Arab-San, you know full well of the tradition of the slaying of the beast. Yes, that is how you are, are you not? You master and you slay. Yes, I know that you understand it as a way to master yourself with grace and charm and courage. But do you love the animal? No, you love only to slay it, and eat it, or sacrifice it.

I cannot say you nay, for I, too, have fought this creature and have longed to slay him. I cannot slay him, for I am slain thereby. I cannot tame him, unless I am tamed. He and I are one. But being one is nothing if I cannot mount his back and walk with him peacefully home, playing the tune upon my flute. That I long to do. That desire is illusion, too, and down and black he goes, and down and black I go too.

Will you listen black-white ox?
WIll the music calm you?
Does your ear harken to its sound?
Or do you fear I'll harm you!

You are right to fear, you know,
For I am blacker still than you.
You are only a beast,
An animal, fancier than me.
But I have a mind that will not be stilled
Deadlier by far than thee.

But we can not be parted:
Neither you from me, nor me from It.
And if I can not be parted from me.
Then neither You from It.
So fear not, oh ox.
For two are one, and three are one
And the saving force of the Buddha is
Upon us.

III

Many days we wandered, the bull and I. Of course we wandered together, for we could no longer be parted. Now I saw him whitening, whitening, and I was joyous. Then I saw his whitening was too white, as if all the life and joy were going out of him, and I grew worried, lest my bull become a cow and just be content to chew the cud all day. At this, my bull laughed. Yes, he laughed indeed. To you it might sound like a snort, since it comes from my bull and not from your own, but to me it was surely a laugh. A great deep laugh, that began in the belly and worked its way up and out. As if he were to say, "Oh, my master, you have tried to tame me and make me good, and now when I am, you grow irritable and think me too tame. Who is it that must be tamed? Hunger of a soul? Or power-tyranny of a master?"

Thus it was that I imagined that my animal spoke to me. I, indeed, could imagine it, could I not? For he was and is the animal of my own soul and who, if not I, can know his language? I listened to the animal of my soul and I ruefully agreed with him. The tamer must be tamed, and if there is no love, there is no point. Thus the flute. Ah, to play a flute without love is impossible, is it not? I played once again, but aside and near him, my ox-bull friend, not astride him.

I did not know why I did not try and ride him once more, but I waited. Then I saw. What did I see? I saw a cat leap upon his back. I saw a man dig a goad into his side. I saw him teased by a cape. All this I saw. Ashes! said I. I have always thought that the whitening of my bull, his taming, has always to do with me. Now I see. There are those others, those cats and goads and people and capes.

My ox-bull does not know what hits him. In a moment, he is snorting and raging and stuck and does not know who has done this to him. Then they say. "What a wild bull! What a vicious fellow! My!" I do not know it either, and lament that it is all my fault. Oh, precious bull, friend of mine! I have forsaken thee. "They" have been able to fool me and thee. Whether they have wanted to or not. Oh, good bull, we must become canny, you and I. The willow on the bank is green, and can just stay that way, but it, too, can be crushed by a boot. Bull, you must see and smell and hear. Ah, now, that is the reason for all those sense organs! Was I blind? Indeed, I was! I thought that all his sense organs had to do with inner vision alone! Ah, what a fool, what a foolish fool of a fool am I! Yes, these senses are to tell him when there are cats and goads and brutes and capes about. It is enough to know that he screams because he has been pierced!

Ah, brave bull! Now we dance, you and I! Let us dance, you on all fours, I on all twos. We dance, for I have discovered it. I have discovered what every fool in the world has already known! Ah, congratulations to me, and now, I will listen to thee, friend Bull. When you snort, I will guess it is because you have been hit!

> Ah, brave bull, you do not speak.
> And because you do not, I am slow to understand.
> And so slow am I, that I am more foolish yet.
> And you go down, and I go down, and we neither of us know.
> What has happened to us both.

When the ox-bull and I completed our dance, I took him down into the world again with me. I was ready to test my new insight and to see if, indeed, I could ride on his back, get off again, and be aware when he was being stabbed.

We walked peacefully into the city, and no one remarked about my bull and myself, for we all have ox-bulls, have we not? We all agree not to pay attention to each other in this regard, do we not? It is all so that no one will really criticize us for our animal souls, is that not true? I believe it to be. It must be added that the ones who criticize most are, in reality, quite unaware of their own animal souls. These, poor things, are either old and dead, like the elders, or have masked their animal souls beyond any hope and thus are resentful that any other animals are alive. Very sad, but painfully true, I think, don't you?

No matter if you agree or not, my ox-bull and I came into the marketplace to see if we could be accepted. Sometimes I did it angrily and badly, sometimes elegantly. Then there were those who shook their capes at him -- they were hungry for games and competitive events. I was tempted to bring out my sword, but realized that that was no longer an issue at all: I had to protect my bull without provoking another and be cat-like, cape-like or goad-like in return -- if I could. Sometimes I could and sometimes, I could not. Ah, was that it? Was I now really so free and detached that I was free of the desire to be non-attached? With that, my bull fell down in the mud, I atop him, and muddy, too. Now I laughed and laughed, and my bull laughed too.

Now see me there, can you? I am walking peacefully in the marketplace atop my ox-bull. I am playing the flute peacefully, and I laugh. Sometimes I laugh, sometimes I cry. Sometimes I am angry, sometimes I am peaceful. The bull falls down and the bull gets up.

I drink when I am thirsty, I eat when I am hungry. Now and then I sleep, and am as lazy as can be. Now and then I have desire, and now and then I hear fear. Fear is what I hear -- or desire is what I hear. But I hear and do not fear -- or rather, I hear fear and hear desire, but I no longer fear desire. Do you know what I mean? Look at the rose! How it grows! Listen to my tune as I walk and sit on the back of my bull.

> Oh! Ox-bull, I love thee.
> Oh! I know thee.
> To sit sweetly upon thy back --
> No reins.
> To quietly walk home --
> No reins.
> Or to fear with thee and
> follow that --
> No reins.
> Your snout turns upward to
> my tune.
> My flute turns downward
> to your rhythm.
> Is it noon, with sun aloft?
> Or night, with moon serene?
> Ah, ox-bull, what does it matter?
> Man and Bull are one.

IV

Now, the animal has gone out of sight, and I sit alone, atop the mountain, looking at the darkening sun and misty moon. Rainy it is, and cloudy. Nature is sad and beautiful. Yes, you surely know how our nature is, for you have seen the paintings of our Masters. Nature copies the paintings of our Masters, does it not?

It is nice, to sit serenely, with whips put away. Now despair has taken me over once again. It is not the animal, poor soul of a bull-ox, who has nagged me and tormented me and driven me and kept me from my peace. No, it is not he. Well, let me say, in fairness, that it is no longer He, this bull-soul of mine. No, not He. Nay, it is me...Yes, yes, yes. It is the I, the me, the one who speaks, in his God-Almightiness. That is the one who puts me in despair.

What a pipsqueak is the little ego, pompously and vainly sitting atop it all. Thinking that it can, or should, lead the animal at all. Yes, the animal has gone out of sight, all right. But the Man is still here, the Man that I am! The vain and stinking man that I am. Ah, this I saw in the Elders. Their vain, pompous, little pretensions, lording over their fellow creatures, as if they knew, at all, what is best for another, or how he should be! Ah, and that awful little creature is, of course, me, too. It is I that is vain, and ambitious, and cruel, and it is, save us all, the "I" that wishes to retreat from the "I".

Let me fall away from myself. Let me bury my head 'neath the mat, 'neath the wood of the pillow. But I cannot escape myself. Wherever I look, I find myself. It is the I who seeks to escape. It is the I that I find when I do escape. It is the I that I see in thee, no matter how I disguise it and change it and move it and account for it.

Oh, give me my sword, for now I know what to do with it! Oh, I must plunge it within -- take it into my belly and rip and put an end to this Me -- this bloated little me. Death, you are not to be feared, you are to be welcomed as the ender of this meaningless and pompous little kabuki drama of mine. Silence! Even my tongue, as it speaks, continues the proclamation of the I. Silence, tongue, Silence! The one who proclaims silence, who demands it, is also the pompous little tyrant. Oh, oh, oh! The groans come out of my belly, as if the sword were already within. The groans are not from pain of the wound, self-inflicted, but are pains that self inflicts them. Where can I flee from self? Where can I go? I follow me everywhere!

Has it always been so? Was it this that Gautama endured? Is it this that leads them to hold up one finger? Or a flower? Or to keep one's finger to one's lips? Or to slap the other in the face? A thousand ways of saying, "Do not ask me, for I do not know! Not only do I not know, but if I were to speak, I would already show that I do not know, and that this pompous little ego of mine is already thinking and proclaiming that it knows." Yes, surely these great and wonderful Masters knew that. The demon of it all is the "I", the little me. No, not your I, but my I. As I say it, I proclaim the specialness of My "I". Oh, pain, oh, agony, oh wounds of the soul much greater than that of the flesh!

Where can I go to escape me? Where can I hide? No use asking the question. For the questioner is always I.

Let me turn to you. If I look at the you, then, perhaps, I escape the I. So, I look at you, and what do I see? Ah, it is already finished, because it is the I that questions what it sees. Even if I were to question it another way, it could only report that it is the it, is the it, is the it, is the it, into an eternity of its that are I's.

So then, if it cannot be escaped, then let us love it. Ha! Now I escape by calling me "us." Like a fancy court. Or a school of swordsmen, all contained within the One that is Me! Oh, your Lordship of Myself, must I now address you as a plural, as a school of Lords? Fine, another way of illusion and self-deception. Oh, most great and glorious and pompous little ego! I bow down before you, for who could possibly be great enough to bow before you and be received by you, than you yourself! It is not enough that I touch my head to the floor to you, I must be totally flattened. There, does that please you? . . .No? It does not? Because it is still only the I that does it? Totally flattened or totally flattered -- it is the same!

Let me run screaming into oblivion!

Will death, then, do it? Will that beloved state dissolve once and for all this sated samurai self which seeks self and self alone? No, surely not. For the wheel of *samsara* will continue. Life after life, *kalpa* after *kalpa*, aeon after aeon, until all karma is dissolved. So, then, pompous little man, if not this ego, then another, and another, and another. Until the sands of time are all piled up on the beach of eternity.

Nothing, then, little Ronin; nothing, then little Samurai; nothing, then, little nothing, except to accept this pompous little ego of yourself. Nothing to do but accept it. What was it that the great Master once said: "One day you will find that the one who needs all your care and love is yourself." Ah, now I see what it is that he meant. That is what he meant, he meant -- that is what he meant. Now, I can sing my song. Shall I sing it? Yes.

The great little "I" shall love
The great little "I" shall love
The great little "I" shall love
The wicked little "I".
The great little "eye" sees the wicked little "I"
The great little "eye" sees the wicked little "I"
The great little "eye" sees the wicked little "I"
It sees and is blind to itself.
The great little "Eye" needs the wicked little "I"
The great little "Eye" needs the wicked little "I"
To see.
The wicked great "Eye" sees the good little "I"
The wicked great "Eye" sees the good little "I"
The wicked great "Eye" sees the good little "I"
And stabs itself with the sword.
Weep not, great Eye. Cry not, little I.
And who is this who says, "Weep not, cry not"?
Is it not another "I"?
No, it is not another "I".
No, it is not. It is not.
Who is it then?
And who is it then, who asks?
It is Nature who asks.
It is Nature who asks.
It is Nature who asks of itself.

I repeat: It is Nature who asks,
It is Nature who asks.
It is Nature who asks
Of itself.
And who is this who says, "I repeat"?
It is "I", of course, it is "I".
Do you understand?
Do you understand?

I do; I do.
Eye do; Eye do.
Aye, do; Aye, do.

And there, way up in the air,
There it is: A circle fair.
Sunyata: Suchness
Mandala: Muchness.
And Man has Gone out of Sight.

V

A tree stands in the forest.
Its trunk arches and bends.
No miracle. All do it.
But see: How one side of trunk

Grew round,
And other side of trunk,
Grew round,
And both meet again,
Making a hole.
A hole, is it?
Or a whole?
An empty nothing of everything,
In the middle of the tree trunk.
And that is what is meant
When we say: The tree is treeing.

A flower sways in the wind.
Its petals hold onto its powder.
Does it love itself?
Like a woman stroking her breasts?
Yes.
As the roots love the ground.
Little roots: fine flower.
Great root: gross flower.
Root of the flower.
Roots of the tree.
They sway and bend and arch.
And seek their Source.
Up into Heaven, down into Earth.

And that is what is meant,
When we say: The flower is flowering.

The painter sees the tree-hole,
Though he is blind.
The painter hears the flower,
Though he is deaf.
The painter smells his art,
Though he has no nose.

He tells us all,
Though he can not speak.
And man is a painter,
Is he not?
And knows the sound of flowers,
The smell of visions,
The words of pictures.

And that is what is meant,
When we say: The painter is painting.

For man is manning
And trees are treeing
And life seeks its goal;

Which is: to be.
The bee is beeing,
Why can't we?

The Source.
It speaks:
Where, in the thunder of the Name,
Is the ghost?
The one who speaks without body?
Does he exist?

Apart from Nature?
No.
Nothing, then is supernatural?
No, all is natural.
And the best must be Super-Natural.
What is most natural, is.

Even anti-natural?
Yes. Even anti-natural.
For nature has its opposites,
Nature *is* its op-o-sits.
Strange word, listen:
Op-look! O-oh! Sits-be!

And that is what is meant,
When we say: nature is naturing.

VI

So I came down from my mountain, and no one knew that I had been away. No one knew at all, at all -- no one knew at all. That, Sir Knight, is a miracle, I grant you. That is the saving force of the Buddha that is upon us.

For when He is with me and I am He, I have bliss-bestowing hands, I walk with my laughing face, and paunchy belly, and I am at home with wine-bibbers, vagabonds, and tramps. As well as warriors and teachers and geishas. And wives and children and ants. We and they are all Buddhas, are we not? Yes, we are. Buddha and his Bo tree, and you and your Tree of Immortality. And I? Yes, I. Now, I walk without a sword. Now I carry a staff, and a lamp, and people come to me for bliss and enlightenment.

What do I tell them? I say, "Go away, there is nothing to know!" For now I know that what the Old Masters have said is true: There is nothing to know. I also know—and this the sad and wonderful part—that we all have to find this out for ourselves and in our own way and in our own time, and many times over, and with many gurus, and with no gurus.

So, come my friends, Sir Knight and Sir Arab, drink with me and embrace me, as I embrace me, as I embrace thee. For my tree is as yours, Sir Knight, and my animal is as yours, Sir Arab. My triangle, too: My self with all its faults and sufferings, the saving force of the Buddha, and Sunyata: the suchness of things. My triangle, too.

Look, look, see!: The Great Circle of the Rising Sun, Setting Moon, and Empty Hole! You see it there in the trunk of the Tree? It can contain your Star, but need not. It can contain your Crescent, but need not. It is all one, as I have said, and we have said. So, my brothers, I salute you as Buddhas!

The Ten Oxherding Pictures of Pu-ming

1. Undisciplined

2. Discipline Begun

3. In Harness

4. Faced Round

5. Tamed

6. Unimpeded

7. Laissez Faire

8. All Forgotten

9. The Solitary Moon

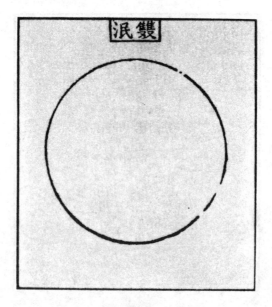

10. Both Vanished

The Ten Oxherding Pictures of Kuo-an

1. Searching for the Ox

2. Seeing the Traces

3. Seeing the Ox

4. Catching the Ox

5. Herding the Ox

6. Coming Home on the Ox's Back

7. The Ox Forgotten

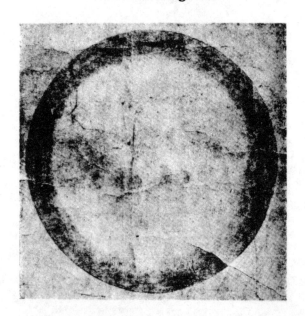

8. The Ox and the Man Both Gone Out of Sight

9. Returning to the Origin

10. Entering the City

Part Three

ASPECTS OF BUDDHISM AND JUNGIAN PSYCHOLOGY

LIVING WITH DUHKHA

By Mokusen Miyuki

On campus in Berkeley a few years ago, I came upon a group of young people with shaved heads and dressed in yellow robes, who were dancing and singing "Hare Krishna." A fair sized audience had gathered, and I questioned one of the campus policemen about the performers. He replied, "Why, they're Buddhists of course! Look at the shaved heads and outfits. They're kids who leave home, don't work, just dance around like this all the time." For me, this reply was a strong reminder of the general understanding of Buddhism in the West. Now, while Hare Krishna practitioners are not Buddhists, this man's impression had some validity in that there have always been two distinct trends in Buddhism: The Buddhist order (samgha) includes both monks and nuns, and lay people. Indeed, it is well know that Theravada monks shave their heads and wear yellow robes, and of course they are much more noticeable than the average lay Buddhist. Therefore, it is not particularly surprising that in the West Buddhism is generally conceived of as an other-worldly Eastern religion.

Contrary to this view of Buddhism is the conception of it as a realistic and pragmatic religion that is oriented to helping the individual constructively deal with real life problems. However, because of Buddhism's teaching of *duhkha*, which unfortunately is often translated as "suffering" or "ills," it is somewhat reasonable

117

that non-Buddhists sometimes interpret Buddhism as pessimistic and life-negating. I would like to deal with the concept of *duhkha*, show that it is at the core of the Buddhist experience, and explain how it is a life-affirming principle.

The Sanskrit word *duhkha* refers to problematic conditions arising from natural processes, and in this sense is descriptive. Etymologically *duhkha* is composed of the prefix *jur* (bad) and the root *kha* ("the hole in the nave of a wheel through which the axis runs," Mornier-Williams, 1899, p. 334). Consequently, the term implies in the wider sense that the "wheel of life" does not run well. Therefore, although *duhkha* is usually translated as "suffering," this translation is misleading for it suggests a merely subjective situation instead of a condition of life. A better translation of *duhkha* would be "disease" because this term conveys the state of man's basic condition, and cuts across the subjective and objective realms of human reality. Huston Smith's explanation of *duhkha* would seem to support this view: "Life in the condition it has got itself into is dislocated. Something has gone wrong. It is slipped out of joint" (1958, p. 112).

The teaching of *duhkha*, or "dis-ease," had its origin in Buddha's experience of life, and it has been formulated in many Buddhist doctrines. Essential to the Buddha's teaching are the Four Noble Truths. In his first sermon (see Rhys-Davids, 1969) Buddha stated that by realizing the Four Noble Truths he became an awakened one. In the First Noble Truth Buddha cites the following human limitations as *duhkha*: birth, old age, sickness, death, sorrow, lamentation and despair, contact with unpleasant things, separation from the one we love, and not getting what we wish. The cause of *duhkha*, which is the Second Noble Truth, refers to the cravings which tie a man to endless cycles of rebirth and death (samsara). The fact that *duhkha* can be overcome by removing the cause, is the Third Noble Truth. This state of being free from craving is known as enlightenment, or *nirvana*, and is the ideal state to be achieved. The way in which one can attain *nirvana* is the Fourth Noble Truth, and this way is described as the Noble Eight-fold Way, namely, right views, right intentions, right speech, right action, right livelihood, right effort, right mindfulness *sati*, and right concentration *samadhi*.

The Four Noble Truths are concerned with the fact no one can change life itself, but that man has the ability to change his attitude and learn to live with his *duhkha*. Dogen (1200-1253), the founder of Soto Zen, said that "Beautiful flowers die because we mourn them, while weeds flourish because we abhor them" (1964, Vol. I, p. 83; see Masunaga, 1958, p. 126). If a man does confront his *duhkha* by seeing reality objectively, then his ego-centered attachment is overcome. In such a situation man then develops a non-ego-centered personality (*anatman*) in which the ego is only a part.

These essential Buddhist teachings are portrayed in the diagram of the Wheel of Life. The Japanese version of the Wheel of Life was engraved and published by a monk named Cho-on during the Tempo era (1830-1844), in accordance with the Vinaya text of Mulasarvastivada Buddhism (see I-Ching). In this picture the Wheel of Life is held in the claws of the devil of impermanence, indicating that the wheel is put into motion by the unavoidable fact of impermanece. The sitting Buddha is depicted in the axle-space of the wheel with a pig, snake, and dove below him. These animals are designated respectively as "full of ignorance," "full of anger," and "full of greed." A personality which is conditioned by these three mind qualities, called the "three poisons" of ignorance, anger and greed, manifests, according to Buddhist thought, in terms of five qualities of life, or realms of beings. In the picture these five qualities are depicted as infernal beings, hungry ghosts, human beings, heavenly beings, and animal beings. In the Tibetan Wheel of Life, which is based on the Sarvastivadin tradition, the fighting spirit is placed between the heavenly beings and animal realm (Khantipalo, 1970; see Govinda, 1969, pp. 234-241).

The axle-space itself symbolizes the core of personality. If this core is dominated by these three animals, or qualities of mind, then the entire personality, is "poisoned," or conditioned by attachment to life situations, thus producing a poorly constructed axle-space, i.e., *duhkha*. The sitting Buddha in the axle-space represents the Buddha-essence, the genunine self, or the total personality; it is at the same time the capacity to realize this authentic being. It relates, therefore, to the infinite potentials of human creativity, as well as to the freedom to create and re-create the genuine self by continually confronting *duhkha* in unique life circumstance. It is because of the Buddha-essence in man that he can liberate himself from attachment, transcend his ego-centered world, and realize his total personality (*anatman*).

The emphasis on man's ability to realize his genuine self by facing the reality of *duhkha* is very strong in the Mahayana tradition, especially in Japanese Buddhism. The Japanese ideal is to cultivate the personality, or state of mind, in which the self-destructive ego-centered forces are positively integrated. The Zen teaching of "no-mind" (*mushin*) and the Shinshu teaching of "naturalness" (*jinen honi*) are both directed to the realization of this total personality and can be considered as examples of the way in which the Japanese mind has transformed the other-worldly Buddhism of India into a pragmatic system for dealing with everyday life.

D.T. Suzuki considered Zen teaching of "no-mind" as the core of the Buddhist spiritual heritage, and sees it as essential to the formation of the Japanese personality or character. In explaining "no-mind" in his work *Zen and Japanese Culture* (1970), Suzuki quotes the following story told by Goso Ho-yen (Fa-yen, died 1104) of the Sung dynasty:

> The son of a burglar saw his father growing older and thought, "If he is unable to carry out his profession, who will be the breadwinner of this family except myself? I must learn the trade." He intimated this to his father, who approved of it.
>
> One night the father took the son to a big house, broke through the fence, entered the house, and opening one of the large chests, told the son to go in and pick out the clothing. As soon as he got into it, the lid was dropped and the lock securely applied. The father now went out to the courtyard, and loudly knocking at the door, woke up the whole family. Then he himself quietly slipped away through the former hole in the fence. The people of the house got excited and lighted candles, but found that the burglar had already gone. The son, who had remained all the time in the chest securely confined, thought of his cruel father.
>
> He was greatly mortified, when a fine idea flashed upon him. He made a noise which sounded like the gnawing of a rat. The family told the maid to take a candle and examine the chest. When the lid was unlocked, out came the prisoner, who blew out the light, pushed away the maid, and fled. The people ran after him, noticing a well by the road, he picked up a large stone and threw it into the water. Trying to find the burglar drowning himself in the dark hole, the pursuers all gathered around the well.
>
> In the meantime the son was safely back in his father's house. He blamed his father very much for his narrow escape. Said the father, "Be not offended, my son. Just tell me how you got off." When the son had told him all about his adventures, the father remarked, "There you are, you have learned the art" (pp. 9-10).

This story conveys that there is nothing tangible to learn if one wishes to realize the genuine self and become the master of one's life. Instead the story shows that it is necessary to activate "no-mind," or the state of mind in which one is free from ego-centricity, in order to release one's creativity and become a total person. Dogen also makes this point by stating:

Simply letting go of my body, as well as my mind, and forgetting them, in this way everything is carried out by the hand of Buddha. If we do this, then without any effort or worries we can be apart from life and death to become Buddha (1964, Vol. III, p. 240; see Masunaga pp. 98-99.

Dogen explains this "letting go" of one's mind and body as "just sitting" *shikan taza*. He emphasizes effortlessness, or being free of ego-centered contrivance, when he states that "in this way everything is carried out by the hand of Buddha."

The Shinshu teaching of "naturalness" (See Suzuki, 1959) is also concerned with realizing that state of being which transcends egocentric fabrications or manipulations. According to Shinran (1175-1262), the founder of Shinshu Buddhism, achieving this state of "naturalness" is the same as rebirth in Amida's Pure Land, and is made possible by Amida's vow to liberate those *duhkha*-ridden people who recite Amida's name wholeheartedly. It is not because of any human effort, or even recitation of Amida's name and sincere desire for rebirth, that causes man's rebirth. The "Other Power," or Amida's vow, which totally transcends human efforts based on ego-centricity, is the cause of man's rebirth, or achieving the state of "naturalness," Therefore, in order to attain the state of "naturalness," just reciting Amida's name *(tada nembutsu)* is emphasized, as in the case of Dogen's "just sitting."

Shinran's "naturalness," Zen's "no-mind," and Dogen's "letting go" all refer to the activation of the genuine self which is free from ego-centered contrivance. This state of freedom from ego-contrivance is also found in the early eighth century Japanese text the *Kojiji* where it is termed the "mind of purity and brightness" *(kiyoki akaki kokoro)*. This indicates a mind which is "pure" in the sense that it is not contaminated by the "dirt" of ego-centricity, and "bright" because it allows the illuminating activity of the otherwise hidden realm of one's being to take place (see Phillippi, 1969, pp. 75, 79).

Cultivation of the state of mind characterized as "bright and pure" was greatly desired by the ancient Japanese in order to foster a feeling of oneness with nature and their fellow beings. Building on this Japanese ideal the Buddhist religion has emphasized cultivation of the non-ego-centered mind in order to face *duhkha*, or dis-ease. Buddhism is thus seen in Japan as a means to achieve "purity of mind" by dealing with the immediate experience of *duhkha*, and therefore Buddhism is considered as a realistic, this worldly, and life-affirming religion.

This version of Buddhism has greatly influenced various

aspects of Japanese life. D.T. Suzuki's works have made Westerners aware of the Buddhist influence in Japanese cultural traditions such as the tea ceremony, flower arranging, Haiku, calligraphy, sumie, Kendo, Judo and archery. In these traditions, what is emphasized is self-discipline (*kokoro no shuyo*), or "cultivation of the mind-attitude" which is free from ego-confinement because of the activation of spontaneity and creativity of the genuine self (see Ross, 1970, pp. 87-180).

For the Japanese, a calm and tranquil attitude of mind, which is achieved through self-discipline, is the basic requirement if one wants to see things as they are, and best cope with the moment. Kishimoto, a noted religious scholar, gives the following example of how this principle operates in Japanese life:

> Suppose a Japanese woman makes a small commotion by falling down on the street. As she struggles to get up, one may notice a faint smile on her face. In spite of her disturbance, she instinctively tries to keep her mind calm and balanced, and to observe the situation objectively. With great effort she tries to say to herself: "What a blunder you are making," and tries to smile at herself. This whole reaction can occur in an instant, because of long cultural tradition (1967, p. 119).

Western people often experience the "inscrutable" smile of the Japanese, or the "poker face," behind which strong and powerful emotions are concealed. This "inscrutable" smile is the result of consciously controlling one's emotional expression, or self-discipline (Kishimoto, 1967. p. 118). In extreme situations the Japanese smile appears to others as not only strange, but even insane. An example of this occurred in the case of a Japanese scholar studying abroad. He received a telegram from Japan and when his hostess asked him what had happened, he replied with a smile, "My wife has passed away." The lady thought that the man had lost his mind due to unbearable grief, but what she did not see was the scholar's trembling hands as he grasped his handkerchief beneath the table when he answered.

A common misunderstanding that occurs among Japanese families in America is in regard to parental response to praise of their children. A friend of the family might say, "Your son must be brilliant," and the parent replies, "*okaga samade*" (thanks to you), "*Do itashi mashite* (not at all) or "*Mama desu*" (he is o.k.). This kind of reply is often confusing to the children involved as such a response sounds dishonest and discouraging, and the child sometimes reacts very negatively and develops the feeling that his parents are not appreciative of his efforts. However, the parent's reaction to praise of his child is not directed to the child, but is geared to not creating any hard feelings among those who are not so fortunate in their children.

In an unfortunate situation, such as a car accident, a Japanese often reacts oddly for Westerners. Even in the case where one is in the right, the Japanese may bow and say, *"Sumimasen,"* which literally means "I am sorry." For the Japanese, the issue is not to judge the situation in terms of right or wrong, but rather to strive to create a favorable emotional atmosphere, and avoid unnecessary conflict. What one implies by saying *"Sumimasen,"* is that both of us are unfortunate to be involved in this car accident, and I am sorry for having a part in causing this ugly "dis-ease." However, such a response may sound like an admission of guilt to Westerners, and thus they might have grounds to win the case if it is taken to court.

In sorrow, the Japanese also tries to control his emotions. In Japan, as a general rule, the patient is not told if he has a terminal illness. The family are informed of the truth, but they try to hide it. However, the patient sometimes learns of his fate anyway. Maruyama (1970) writing of people hospitalized because of cancer, found that those patients who knew that they had a terminal illness did not want to let the family know that they were aware of their condition. They tried to behave as naturally as possible so that the family would not detect that they knew of their approaching death and needlessly suffer because of their helplessness in the matter. In such a situation the ideal is to face death as inevitable, take it as a challenge, and make the illness an opportunity for further growth.

For the Japanese, living meaningfully and positively until death is believed to be made possible by the attitude one takes. Kishimoto (1962, 1964A, 1946B), who left a record of his own experience with a terminal illness, tells of how he overcame his desperate "hunger for life." He maintained that the only way to prepare for death is based on training the mind to remain calm. He wrote that he came to think of death as a "time of parting" with life, and that he continually prepared mentally to confront death at any moment, with a self-composed attitude of calmly bidding farewell to his life. Thus, whenever he said goodbye to others, he tried to experience that moment as if it had been the last opportunity for him to exchange these words. For him this attitude was the only way to assuredly create meaning and value in his life, and while he still suffered, he was no longer desperate. He even said that he was thankful for his illness as it made him live fully when he otherwise might have idled his life away.

Buddhism and Jungian Psychology

124

In conclusion, I would like to reiterate that Buddhism has often been misuderstood as pessimistic, largely because of its emphasis on *duhkha* which has been translated as "suffering." However, etymologically and dogmatically, *duhkha* is better translated as "disease." The doctrine of *duhkha* has been essential in shaping the Japanese mind in terms of the attitude one needs to achieve when confronting "dis-ease" in life. This attitude, which involves self-discipline, or cultivation of a non-ego-centered personality, is referred to in Zen as "no-mind" and in Shinshu as "naturalness," and penetrates all aspects of Japanese life. From the Buddhist viewpoint, therefore, Buddhism is a realistic and this-wordly religion that sees man as capable of facing his *duhkha* and creating a more meaningful life.

REFERENCES

Dogen. *The Shobogenzo*, 3 vols. Tokyo: Iwanami, 1904, 12th printing.

Govinda, Lama Anagarika. *Foundations of Tibetan Mysticism*. New York: Samuel Weiser, Inc. 1969. Pp. 234-241.

I-Ching. Tr., *Ken-pen shuo i-ch'ieh yo-pu p'i-na yeh*, in *Taisho Daizokyo* XXIII. Pp. 810-811.

Khantipalo, Bhikku. *The Wheel of Birth and Death*. Kandy, Ceylon: Buddhist Publication Society, 1970.

Kishimoto Hideo. *Hitotsu no senkoku (A Final Sentence)*, Zaike Bukkyo (*The Layman's Buddhism*), No. 100, 1962. Pp. 52-57.

Kishimoto Hideo. "My View of Life and Death," *Contemporary Religions in Japan*, Vol. V, No. 2. (June, 1964A). Pp. 107-118.

Kishimoto Hideo, et. al. *Nihinjin no Shiseikan*. (The Japanese View of Death and Life), *Zaike Bukkyo*, (*The Layman's Buddhism*), No. 117. 1964B. Pp. 46-63.

Kishimoto, Hideo. "Some Japanese Cultural Traits and Religions," In *The Japanese Mind*. Edited by Charles A. More. East-West Center, University of Hawaii, Honolulu, 1967

Maruyama, Katushisa. *Ikiru (To Live)*, *Zaike Bukkyo*, No. 194. 1970. Pp. 45-55.

Masunaga, Reiho. *The Soto Approach to Zen*. Tokyo: Layman Buddhist Society Press, 1958. Pp. 98-99, 126.

Mornier-Williams, Sir Morniel. *A Sanskrit-English Dictionary*. Oxford: The Clarendon Press, 1899.

Philippi, Donald L. *Kojiki*. Princeton University Press, University of Tokyo Press, 1969.

Ross, Nancy Wilson. *The World of Zen.* New York: Dover Publications, Inc., 1969. Pp. 87-180.

Rhys-Davids, T.W. *Buddhist Suttas.* New York: Dover Publications, Inc., 1969. Pp. 137-155.

Smith, Huston. *The Religions of Man.* New York: Harper & Row, Publishers, 1958.

Suzuki, D. I. *Mysticism: Christian and Buddhist.* New York: Harper & Brothers Publishers, 1959.

Suzuki, D.T. *Zen and Japanese Culture* (4th ed.). Princeton: Princeton University Press, 1970.

THE IDEATIONAL CONTENT OF THE BUDDHA'S ENLIGHTENMENT
A Jungian Approach
By Mokusen Miyuki

The *dharma* of Interdependent Origination (*pratityasamutpada*)[1] has traditionally been accepted in Buddhism as the ideational content of the Buddha's enlightenment. This teaching is based on those accounts which indicate that it was the most profound of the Buddha's realizations.[2] Also supporting this teaching are those canons which, while not specifically stating that Interdependent Origination is the content of the Buddha's enlightenment, infer it by relating that this *dharma* experienced by the Buddha is too profound and unfathomable to teach.[3] However, in seeming contradiction to this traditional teaching there also exist those canons which give one of the other major teachings of Buddhism, such as the Four Noble Truths, the Noble Eightfold Way, or the Middle Path, as the content of enlightenment.[4]

These inconsistencies could be accounted for, in part, as the product of various sectarian traditions, but this issue can also be considered from a psychological standpoint: All human experience is essentially psychological, in the sense that immediate "reality" is perceived and apprehended in and through our psyches, therefore the experience of enlightenment, and its ideational content, can validly be examined from a psychological perspective as a consequence of efforts to convey an experience which is indescribable from a rational or intellectual standpoint. Furthermore, from this psychological position, the major teachings of Buddhism can then be regarded not as distinct doctrines, but rather as mutual amplifications of an ineffable experience. As such, the essential teachings of Buddhism can be subjected to phenomenological analysis through the use of the methodology and structure of Jungian Analytical Psychology.

As a psychologist, C.G. Jung regarded religion as based on an experience of the numinous. He maintained that religious practice or ritual, such as invocation, incantation, or meditation, aims at producing an encounter with the numinous.[5] As an empiricist and phenomenologist Jung was concerned with the observation and description of the psychological aspects of such numinous experiences as those produced by the Buddha's *dhyana* practice. *Dhyana*-meditation can be understood as a practice or means for creating an experience of the numinous and the Buddha's enlightenment is said to have occurred as he sat in *dhyana*.

Since a numinous experience can not be conceptually formulated or intellectually understood, a person who wishes to share it with another is at a loss for a means of logical communication. One who has had the experience, such as a Zen master, may make an effort to convey or impart the experience by using gestures, a specific tone of voice, or even by resorting to physical violence. Also, he may cite familiar materials which appeal to intuition or feeling, but he will not be able to explain the experience intellectually.

Unconscious materials, such as the contents of a numinous experience, have no conscious language adequate for clarifing their meaning. This lack of an appropriate language occurs because unconscious materials are a psychic phenomenon alien to the conscious mind through which they are communicated. Jung has observed that unconscious contents, because their nature is unknown, have a tendency to self-amplification, that is to say, "they form the nuclei for an aggregation of synonyms."[6] He states: "When something is little known, or ambiguous, it can be envisaged from different angles, and then a multiplicity of names is needed to express its peculiar nature."[7] These synonyms are images which are unmistakably mythological in their character, and Jung regards them as the expression of "the inborn language of the psyche and its structure,"[8] or "the language of the unconscious which lacks the intentional clarity of conscious language."[9] This archaic, non-rational language of the psyche is universally found in such unconscious materials as dreams, fantasies, psychotic episodes, fairy tales, mythology, or religious literature, such as the various accounts of Buddha's experience of the numinous.

Jung states that when dealing with unconscious materials, "we are . . .obliged to adopt the method we would use in deciphering a fragmentary text or one containing unknown words: We examine the context."[10] Jung has termed his method of dealing with unconscious materials "amplification." He maintains that "amplification is always appropriate when dealing with some dark experience which is so vaguely adumbrated that it must be enlarged and expanded by being set in a psychological context in order to be understood at all."[11]

Jung's method of amplification aims at activation of an "insight" into the nature and essence of the psychic process. This insight is accomplished by examining the images or ideas produced by a psychological situation with the help of associated materials drawn from parallels found in other unconscious materials. The images thus amplified, which are otherwise obscure and confusing, can become clearer and more intelligible by being permitted, in a sense, to speak for themselves. The method of amplification cannot attempt to establish or designate the specific content of a numinous experience; it can, however, approximately reveal the essential nature of the experience. An example of amplification is found in the Buddha's first sermon in which he expounds his major teachings as an inseparable continuum; he uses each of the doctrines to amplify the other, and employs all of them as expressions of the numinous experience, or his "profound awakening."[12]

The experience of the numinous can be regarded from a Jungian viewpoint as a confrontation with the archetype of the self. Archetypes are "a formative principle of instinctual power which universally condition human behaviour and perception."[13] They are part of the collective, or inherited psyche, and consist of forms that can never be made wholly conscious although they are approximately represented by mythologems or recurring themes consisting of images and symbols expressed in myths, dreams, folklore, and religious experience. Central to the total psyche is the archetype of the self. Jung states, "the self is not only the center but also the whole circumference which embraces both conscious and unconscious; it is the centre of the totality, just as the ego is the centre of the conscious mind."[14]

Confrontation with the archetype of the self is both mysterious and powerful as well as incomprehensible to the conscious personality which is ego-bound and thing-bound. Such an experience produces a state of introversion in which "a withdrawal of the centre of psychic gravity from ego consciousness" occurs, and the energy thus invested in the unconscious produces a new pattern

of psychic functioning which is not centered around ego consciousness.[15] This state of consciousness, which can be characterized as
being free from ego-orientation, one in which consciousness is
transcending its ego condition.[16] In this non ego-bound mental
condition of the introverted mind, the individual may experience
the insight which can bring about a transformation or renewal of
the entire personality. The transformed personality that is
produced by this confrontation with the archetype of the self or
the numinous experience, is structured around the operation of
the ego/self axis, as opposed to the ordinary ego dominated
personality.

Jung has observed that in the numinous experience, or the
confrontation with the self, mandala symbolism often emerges in
the manifested unconscious materials. A mandala is a symmetrical
structure consisting of ternary or quaternary combinations symbo-
lizing the dynamic process of development or growth, whereas the
quaternary configurations represent a static structural wholeness,
or completion.[17]

The ternary and quaternary number symbolism manifested in
mandalas can be seen as an expression of the emergence of the
renewed personality built on the ego/self axis. As a part of the
psychic process, the ego/self axis actualizes in terms of a ternary
rhythm: differentiation of that which is non-ego is the basis of ego
consciousness. In the case of the transformed or renewed personality,
structured on the ego/self axis, the ego recognizes the self as
non-ego or its opposite. The tension thus created by this duality is
released in the creation of a third mode of being in which the
ego/self interacts. Jung maintains that this psychological process
goes on to be resolved in a "fourth" condition: "The unspeakable
conflict posited by duality resolves itself in a fourth principle. The
rhythm is built up in three steps, but the resultant symbol is a
quaternity."[18]

The ternary and quaternary number symbolism in mandalas is
further elaborated upon by G. Adler:

> So far as the sequence "1,2,4" is concerned it represents the
> development of the mandala symbols, and of psychic totality.
> The number 1 represents an original preconscious totality; 2
> is the division of this pre-conscious totality into two polarites,
> producing two opposites ... And the further subdivision -
> corresponding to the synthesis arising out of thesis and
> antithesis - would produce the four parts of the circle, and
> with its center, signifying the mandala. The sequence of the
> three numbers 1,2,4, would thus represent the natural growth,
> the "formula" of the mandala.[19]

As expressions of the ideational content of the Buddha's experience of the numinous, the essential teachings of Buddhism repeatedly employ in their formulation the mandalic combinations of the numbers 3 and 4. In the doctrine of the Twelve Links of the Chain of Interdependent Origination, the number 12 (3x4) symbolizes the simultaneous occurrence of the process and the goal, or *dhyana-prajna*.

The dual awareness of the *samsaric-nirvanic* life which is expressed in the doctrine of Interdependent Origination, and which is pointedly reinforced in the *Mahavagga's* account of the Buddha's enlightenment[20] by the statement that the Buddha thought over Interdependent Origination both forward and backward,[21] is also clearly stressed in the following formulation of the doctrine:

> When this is, that is;
> This arising, that arises;
> When this is not, that is not;
> This ceasing, that ceases.[22]

Symbolically interpreted, "this" and "that" represent all, or any, possible opposites, such as *samsara* and *nirvana*. In a confrontation with the numinous, or enlightenment, *samsara* and *nirvana* are experienced as the *unus mundus* or interconnected dependency, and this synthesis is the resolution of the duality of the *samsara-nirvana* opposition. Psychologically, to take in "this" and "that" "as-they-are" means that the duality arising from these opposites is transcended on a higher level, or unitary form of consciousness which represents the "third" in the psychic process. Thus, out of the two-ness of the opposites of *samsara-nirvana*, or arising and ceasing, or this and that, comes the three-ness of their synthesis, or the *dharma* of Interdependent Origination.

This simultaneous affirmation, or synthesis of the opposites is, psychologically, the transcendence of the boundary between "I" and the "world." The transcendence of this boundary can be understood to occur as the result of what Jung terms the "transcendent function." The transcendent function is a creative expression of the psyche. It is called "transcendent" because it "facilitates the transition from one psychic condition to another by means of the mutual confrontation of the opposites," namely, conscious and unconscious.[23] The state of consciousness which is produced by transcendence of the opposites is experienced without losing the awareness of the transcendence that occurs. This state of awareness of transcendence is thus the fourth stage of the completion of the psychic process, or enlightenment.

The transcended state of consciousness created by the actualization and activity of the ego/self axis in the enlightenment experience also finds expression in other major teachings in Buddhism. Combinations of the numbers 3 and 4, which psychologically represent growth and development, respectively, appear in the doctrine of the Middle Path. The Buddha, in his first sermon, states that he realized the "Enlightenment of the Middle Path," avoiding two extremes of "self indulgence" and "self mortification."[24] Thus, the Middle Path indicates an on-going process which out of the tension produced by the two extremes is resolved in the Middle Path or the third stage. "Enlightenment of the Middle Path" is the expression of the fourth stage, or the on-going experience of *prajna*.

The realization of the Four Noble Truths is expounded by the Buddha in his first sermon in terms of the Three Sections and Twelve Divisions (*ti-parivattam dvadasakaram*).[25] The Three Sections constitute the process of realization which consists of (1) coming to an awareness of the truth, (2) deciding to practice the truth, and (3) having accomplished this practice. The realization of each of the Four Noble Truths by the practice of these Three Sections, or that of the Twelve Divisions (3x4), results in the attainment of the "ineffable knowledge of things as they have become (*yathabhutam nana-dassanam*), which is a phrase used to designate the experience of enlightenment. Thus, we see in this formulation the reflection of the ternary growth process resolving itself into the quaternary wholeness or completion of enlightenment.

The teachings of the Three Characteristics of *Dharma* is a ternary expression of the process involved in the attainment of enlightenment.[26] Realization of the three aspects of *dharma*, i.e., impermanence (*annica*), dis-ease (*dukkha*), and no-separate entity (*anatta*), leads to the fourth state, or *prajna*.

Another important Buddhist doctrine is the Seven Factors of Enlightenment (*satta bojjhanga*). This teaching combines the numbers 3 and 4 to show the activation of the self in its dynamic, developmental phase in the first three factors of mindfulness (*sati*), discerning the truth (*dhamma-vicaya*), and energy (*viriya*), and the static aspect of completion or realization in the last four factors of rapture (*piti*), serenity (*passaddhi*), concentration (*samadhi*), and equanimity (*upekkha*).

The quaternary teaching of the Noble Eightfold Way can be replaced or interchanged with the ternary formulation of the doctrine of the Threefold Studies.[27] According to Nagarjuna, the Threefold Studies condenses the Noble Eightfold Way as follows: right speech, right conduct and right livelihood are self-training or observance of *sila*; right mindfulness and right contemplation are self-purification or the practice of *samadhi*; right view, right thought and right efforts are self-liberation or *panna*.[28] Herein we can see the dynamic development aspect of the Threefold Studies resolved in the accomplishment of the Noble Eightfold Way, or the quaternary (4+4) formulation of enlightenment. Through this examination of the number symbolism employed in the major teachings of Buddhism we can see that, from a psychological viewpoint, the ideational content of enlightenment can be viewed as an unceasing mutual confrontation of the opposites, or the duality of conscious and unconscious, or ego and self, which resolves itself in a transcended state of consciousness as the third stage of the psychic process, and is accompanied by an awareness of this transcendence as a fourth stage, or enlightenment.

FOOTNOTES

1. The Sanskirt word *pratitya-samutpada* is variously translated in English as follows: "Dependent Origination" - H.C. Warren, *Buddhism in Translation* (New York: Atheneum, Sixth Printing, 1973), p. 82; "The Law of dependent-together origination" - Th. Stscherbatsky, *The Conception of Buddhist Nirvava* (Shanghai: 1940), p. 8; "Dependent Production" - J. Takakusu, *The Essentials of Buddhist Philosophy* (Honolulu: University of Hawaii, 1947), p. 30; "Conditioned Genesis" - W. Rahula, *What the Buddha Taught*) New York: Grove Press, 1962), p. 52; "The Law of Dependent Origination" - A.K. Coomaraswamy, *Buddha and the Gospel of Buddhism* (New York: Harper Torchbooks, 1964), p. 96; etc. However, etymologically speaking, the term *pratitya-samutpada* consists of *pratitya* and *samutpada*. *Pratitya* is a gerund derived from *prati-i* which means "to go towards or against," and thus it means "dependent on, based on." *Samutpada* is a noun derived from the verb *sam-ut-pad* which means "to spring up together, be brought forth or born of . . ." (Refer to Sir M. Mornier-Williams, *Sanskrit English Dictionary* - Oxford: The Clarenton Press, 1899). The term, therefore, means "origination by dependence of one thing on another," (Refer to Franklin Edgerton, *Buddhist Hybrid Sanskrit Grammar and Dictionary* Vol. II - New Haven: Yale University Press, 1953, p. 373) and indicates the "phenomenon" of the dynamic mutual interdependence of each and every *dharma*.

2. See the following texts for examples: *The Mahavagga* in the opening sections. An English translation of this canon is found in H.C. Warren, *Buddhism in Translation* (New York: Atheneum Press,

1963), pp. 83-85. *The Nidanakatha* (Introduction to the *Jataka*), a partial translation of this text is found in H.C. Warren *op. cit* pp. 12-46. On the basis of this text, H. Kern presents the life of the Buddha in his *Manual of Indian Buddhism* (Varanasi, India: Indological Book House, 1968). *THe Buddha-carita of Asvaghosha*, translated by E.B. Cowell in *The Sacred Books of the East* Vol. XLIX (London: OXford University Press, 1894), Part I. *Kuo-chu hsien-tsui yin-kuo ching* in the *Taisho* III, 620, No. 189. Translated by Gunabhadra in 444-453 A.D. This text was widely circulated in China and Japan.

3. See, for instance the *Mahasaccaka-sutta* in the *Majjhima-nikaya* I, 240ff. This canon states that the Buddha recalled his experience of *sati*, or mindfulness, under the rose-apple tree and thought that it was the way to enlightenment. Nevertheless, the Buddha after having attained enlightenment is said to have hesitated to preach because he thought mankind would find it difficult to see the truth of Interdependent Origination.

4. Those canons that do relate the content of the Buddha's enlightenment vary greatly. In certain texts, such as the *Vinaya* text of the *Mulasarvastivadin* (*Ken-pen shuo i-ch'ieh yu-pu p'i-na-yeh p'o-seng shih* in *Taisho* XXIV, No. 1450, p. 124b), or the *Vinaya* text of Dharmagupta (*Ssu-fen lu* in *Taisho* XXII, No. 1428, p. 781c), etc., the Four Noble Truths are considered as the content of the Buddha's enlightenment. In the First Sermon, however, not only the Four Noble Truths but also the Middle Path and the Noble Eightfold Way can be considered as the content of the Buddha's enlightenment. (The First Sermon is found in *Samyutta-nikaya* v. 420).

5. C.G. Jung, *Psychology and Religion: West and East. The Collected Works of C.G. Jung* (hereafter abridged as CW), Vol. 11, p. 7.

6. C.G. Jung, *Mysterium Coniunctionis.* CW 14, p. 458.

7. C.G. Jung, *Psychology and Religion: West and East.* CW 11, p. 501.

8. C.G.Jung, *Civilization in Transition.* CW 10, p. 339.

9. *Ibid.*, p. 388.

10. C.G.Jung, *Psychology and Alchemy.* CW 12, p. 44.

11. *Ibid.*, p. 277.

12. In the First Sermon, the Buddha states that he has attained "the enlightenment of the Middle Path (*majjhima patipada*)"; thus, we are given the impression that the Middle Path is the content of his enlightenment. He then equates the Middle Path with the Noble Eightfold Way and goes on to expound the Four Noble Truths, emphasizing the realization of the Four Noble Truths, in terms of the Three Sections and Twelve Divisions (*ti-parivattam dvadasakaram*). In this canon, therefore, any one of the three teachings, i.e., the Middle Path, the Noble Eightfold Way, or the

Four Noble Truths, can duly be considered as the content of the Buddha's enlightenment.

13. C.G. Jung, *The Structure and Dynamics of the Psyche.* CW 8, p. 212.

14. C.G.Jung, *Psychology and Alchemy.* CW 12, p. 41.

15. C.G. Jung, *Psychology and Religion: West and East.* CW Vol. 11, p. 485.

16. *Ibid.*, p. 484.

17. E.F. Edinger, *Ego and Archetype* (Baltimore, Maryland: Penguin Books Inc., 1973). p. 188.

18. C.G. Jung, *Psychology and Religion: West and East.* CW Vol. 11, p. 175.

19. G. Adler, *The Living Symbol* (New York: Pantheon, 1961), p. 29f.

20. The Twelve Links of Interdependent Origination, which are the causes or conditions of *dukkha*, are given in the *Mahavagga*, and in many other accounts, as: ignorance (*avijja*), karmic force (*sankhara*), consciousness (*vinnana*), name and form (*nama-rupa*), the six organs of sense (*salayatana*), contact (*phasso*), sensation (*vedana*), desire (*tanha*), attachment (*upadana*), existence (*bhava*), birth (*jati*), old age and death.

21. The phrase "forward and backward" indicates that the Buddha considered not only the causes or conditions from which the *samsaric* life of dis-ease (*dukkha*) arises (forward), but also he considered the way to overcome or remove the causes of dis-ease (backward) so as to attain *nirvana*.

22. Walpola Rahula's translation. See his *What the Buddha Taught* (New York: Grove Press, 1962), p. 53. This is a set verse which is often, though not always, used in connection with the teachings of the Twelve Links of Interdependent Origination, and which is to be considered as an older formulation of the teaching than that of the Twelve Links. See Nakamura Hajime, "Engi Setsu no Genkei (The Original Formula of the teaching of Interdependent Origination)" in the *Indogaku Bukkyogaku Kenkyu* (Journal of Indian and Buddhist Studies), Vol, 5, No. 1 (1957), pp. 59-68, especially pp. 61-62.

23. C.G. Jung, *Psychology and Religion: West and East.* CW Vol. 11, p. 489.

24. The First Sermon is found in the *Samyutta-nikaya* v. 420.

25. The Four Noble Truths are the essential message of the Buddha's first sermon and have been considered as the pillar of Theravadan teachings. They are: The Noble Truth of Dis-ease (*dukkha*), the Noble Truth of the Uprising-together (*samudaya*) of Dis-ease, and the Noble Truth of the Cessation (*nirodho*) of Dis-

ease, and the Noble Truth of the Path (*maggo*) leading to the cessation of Dis-ease.

26. See, for example, the *Anguttara-nikaya* III, 134.

27. As the Way leading to the cessation of dis-ease, the Noble Eightfold Way is enumerated as follows: right view (*samma-ditthi*), right thought (*samma-sankappo*), right speech (*samma-vaca*), right conduct (*samma-kammanto*), right livelihood (*samma ajivo*), right efforts (*samma-vayam*), right mindfulness (*samma-sati*), and right contemplation (*samma-samadhi*).

28. See the *Ta chih-ta lun* in *Taisho* XXV, No. 1509, p. 488a.

THE PURE LAND
PRACTICE OF NIEN—FO
A Jungian Approach
By Mokusen Miyuki

Asian religions have been interpreted in the West by utilizing extant philosophical religious categories. These categories are rooted in a *Weltanschauung* that is foreign, if not antithetical, to the Asian Culture. Consequently, serious misunderstandings have arisen regarding the nature of Asian religions and thus a tradition such as Buddhism is often seen in the West as pessimistic and life-negating, even to the point of advocating the dissolution of the ego.

C.G. Jung's Analytical Psychology provided the West with the first meaningful approach to the Asian religious experience. Jung's perceptive statements about Eastern religions reveals the depth and richness of the insights afforded him by his empirical and phenomenological methodology. However, Jung remained faithful to his methodology and refrained from coming to decisive conclusions concerning the psychological aspects of religious experience in the East. It is understandable though that others less fortunate than Jung with his unique experience and wisdom have employed Jung's methodology to arrive at some questionable assertions about Asian religions.

The issue I wish to raise at this time involves the prevailing psychological view of Eastern religions as aiming at the "dissolution," or at least the "depotentiation of the ego."[1] I must challenge this conception; for, in my understanding, the Buddhist tradition aids the individual to strengthen the ego through the integration of unconscious contents. Here I will use the Pure Land Buddhist practice of *nien-fo* as an example of an Eastern religious practice that develops the ego/self axis.

The religious practice of *nien-fo*, or what is today in the Pure Land tradition recitation of the Amida Buddha's name, grew out of the need for a religious practice that laymen could incorporate into their daily lives. This movement towards a secularization of Buddhism occurred during the T'ang dynasty, around the seventh century A.D., and the initiator of this development was the Pure Land master Shan-tao (613-681). A few centuries later, in Kamakura, Japan, Honen (1133-1212), founder of the Japanese Pure Land tradition, and his disciple Shinran (1173-1262), based their teachings about *nien-fo* on the writings of the Chinese master Shan-tao.

The Chinese term *nien-fo* is composed of two words, *nien* which has several meanings, and *fo* meaning Buddha. *Nien* has been used as a translation of the Sanskrit term *smriti* and the Pali word *sati*. Both *smriti* and *sati* refer to concentrating on the immediate feeling or thinking process. Hence, *nien-fo* denotes concentrating on the visual image of the Buddha in all its splendor. A further meaning inherent in this use of *nien* is the idea of transcending the visual image and meditating on the essence of Buddha's being (*dharma-kaya*). These two definitions specify *nien-fo* as *samadhi* or meditation practice, however, the term *nien* also carries the meaning of recitation. Thus *nien-fo* in the Pure Land tradition indicates a verbal/mental recitation of the name of the Amida Buddha.

According to the Pure Land, or Mahayana, pantheon there are innumerable Buddhas or Awakened Ones. The myth of the Amida Buddha, or Amitabha, tells of a king whose most fervent desire was for the happiness and well being of the people in his kingdom.[3] Eventually this king realized that no matter how much he tried to help people, material well being was not enough for real happiness. Thus, he became a monk and journeyed to see the Buddha Lokesvararaja who told him that by his own efforts he should create a land wherein sentient beings could find utmost happiness.

For five *kalpas*, or an immense amount of time, the monk meditated on what kind of land he wanted to create. Finally he decided and made forty-eight vows in order to accomplish this creation. To fulfill these vows he practiced inconceivable perfection for a measureless amount of time. He now dwells in the western quarter of his land of utmost happiness were he welcomes all sincere practitioners.

In the Japanese Pure Land tradition, the practice of *nien-fo* is known as *nembutsu* and is based on the Amitabha's eighteenth vow. This vow states:

> Upon my attainment of Buddahood, should the sentient beings in the ten quarters who have sincerity of heart (*shih-hsin*), who rejoice in the faith (*hsin-lo*), and who wish for rebirth into my land (*yu-sheng wo-kua*), if they, while repeating my name and directing their thoughts to me up to ten times, are not to be born therein, then may I not attain Buddhahood.[4]

Shan-tao, a prominent Buddhist master of the early T'ang dynasty interpreted and practiced *nien-fo* according to Amitabha's eighteenth vow. He held that *nien-fo* is the essential teaching of the Pure Land faith and is called "the right and decisive karma for rebirth into the Pure Land (*cheng-ting-shih-yeh*) because it is in accordance with the Buddha's vow."[5] Shan-tao emphasizes that one should recite the Buddha's name throughout one's lifetime, but if one recites it for even one to seven days, or even for one moment, it is adequate for rebirth because of the Buddha's vow. He states:

> It is necessary to devote oneself constantly to the mental/verbal recitation of Amitabha's name with a singleness of purpose (*i-hsin*), and to not abandon this practice at any time either in walking, dwelling, sitting, or lying down, and to practice without regard for the length of time one practices.[6]

Shan-tao's most important teachings are in the form of a commentary on the Pure Land canon, the *Kuan Wu-liang-shou-fo ching*. In this commentary he elucidates the practice of *nien-fo* by using a parable. The parable of The White Path and the dreams which he relates in the postscript of this commentary clarify the psychological nature of *nien-fo* practice and reveals its ego-strengthening nature.

Shan-tao's first dream occurs in relation to his preparation for writing the commentary on the *Kuang-ching*. He states that before he began writing he paid homage to the Buddha and the innumerable bodhisattvas and requested that they give him approval in the form of a dream if his views were in accordance with their vows and intentions. After having made this request in front of Buddha's image, he chanted the *A-mi-to ching* three times, and the name of Amitabha thirty-thousand times with "a sincere mind and honest intentions."[7] That very night he dreamed of the Pure Land in the western sky in all its glory. He relates that in the dream "treasure mountains of many colors are piled up hundred-fold and thousand-fold. Multi-colored lights shine on the ground below. The ground appears to be of gold and sitting or standing there are many Buddhas and Bodhisattvas. Some of the company are talking while others are silent, and some are moving their bodies and hands while others are dwelling immovable. Seeing this sight, I pay reverence while observing it."[8]

Upon awakening, Shan-tao rejoiced in his vision and felt encouraged to begin his commentary. He further stated that, while he was writing the first part of the commentary, a divine monk appeared every night in his dreams and instructed him in its composition.[9]

We can see that in this situation Shan-tao's *nien-fo* practice aimed at an immediate experience of the numinous. His request for guidance in the form of a dream led to the numinous mandala dream he relates and his encounter with the self. Strengthening the ego is of primary importance in preparing for an encounter with the numinous. Such a direct confrontation with the numinous as that had by Shan-tao could possibly cause the disintegration of the personality. However, whereas the Westerner prepares for this numinous experience through a conscious attempt to integrate unconscious contents, the Eastern tradition readies the individual for this experience with religious rituals and meditation-practices such as *nien-fo*.

Jung regarded religion as based on an experience of the numinous. He maintained that religious practice or ritual, such as invocation, incantation, or meditation aims at producing an encounter with the numinosity of the self.[10] In the religious practice of *nien-fo* what takes place is the rearrangement of psychic conditions which can consequently result in a new psychic pattern of functioning. Thus, in Shan-tao's situation he gained through *nien-fo* practice the confidence to assert his own views regarding the importance of *nien-fo* and for the first time opened up such a practice to laity and clergy alike.

Psychologically viewed, *nien-fo* is a means to create, as a Zen koan does, "an almost perfect lack of conscious assumptions."[11] This means that the withdrawal of the center of psychic gravity centered around the ego takes place and is followed by the creation of a new psychic condition that is not ego-centric but ex-centric, meaning that the center of the consciousness is in a state of flux. In the ex-centric state of mind one can experience a spontaneous interplay of images, visions, feelings and ideas which are partially related to past experience. Therefore one can experience his present condition in various ways by integrating these psychic contents and in this way man can expand or enlarge his awareness and thus strengthen his ego-orientation.

This ex-centric state of mind has been characterized in the Buddhist tradition as *anatta* or *anatman*. These terms have been variously translated, without an awareness of the psychological implications involved, as "non-ego," "no-self," "without self," "no soul" and "lacking in Ego."[12] The terms "non-ego," "no-self," etc., are inadequate translations of the ideas expressed in the term *anatman* and such translations serve to further confuse what is a difficult concept to place in Western categories. Perhaps this lack of an appropriate category in which to place the concept of *anatman* led to the misunderstandings in the West about the nature of the Buddhist experience.

The term *anatman* consists of the prefix *an* which means "not," and *atman* which has been analyzed etymologically in two different ways. Some scholars hold that the root word is the verb *an* which means "to breathe," and others maintain that the root verb is *at*, meaning "to walk." Either root denotes a principle of life, and the suffix *man* is a gerund that makes the root an action word. Thus the concept of *atman* indicates a dynamic process of growing or changing, and consequently *anatman* refers to the idea of not identifying oneself with any one aspect of being, but rather envisioning one's being as more than the parts that make up the whole, or as a constantly changing process/state. It is, therefore, a serious misunderstanding to apply western categories and identity *atman* as a separate entity such as ego, self or soul.

In the Second Sermon of the Buddha, which was addressed to those monks who had already gained enlightenment, the Buddha stated that to identify one's *atman* with any part of phenomenal existence, either inner or outer, causes dis-comfort (*dukkha*) because all psycho-physical realities including one's body, feelings, perceptions, consciousness and volition are always in change.[13] What he communicates is the idea that one should not create an illusory identity because man can become more than what his ego-centric consciousness makes him. Buddha's discussion of the importance of *anatman* was directed towards those who had already experienced ex-centric consciousness. Therefore, early scriptures maintained that to understand impermanence, discomfort and *anatman*, or the Three Characteristics of Dharma, is only possible for those who already have *sati* consciousness.

The teaching of *anatman* thus aims at helping the individual to dispel his erroneous identity created by ego-centric consciousness and experience the genuine self. In his discussion of the *Kuang-ching,* Jung writes of how the Buddhist arrives at the experience of the genuine self:

> In order to attain this final goal it was necessary to pass
> through all the laborious exercises of mental reconstruction,
> to get free of the deluded ego-consciousness which is responsible
> for the sorrowful illusion of the world, and to reach that other
> pole of the psyche where the world as illusion is abolished.[14]

This process of dispelling the illusory identity and manifesting
the true self cannot be identified with aiming at dissolution of the
ego. On the contrary, the ego functions in conjunction with the
self in creating a state of constant renewal and enrichment. Such a
process Jung refers to as living the symbolic life or individuation.

Shan-tao's parable of The White Path can be understood as an
effort to communicate that *nien-fo* practice enables one to live the
symbolic life or create the ego/self axis to experience the genuine
self. The parable of The White Path is as follows:

> There is a man who desires to travel a hundred thousand ris
> towards the west. When he is halfway along in his journey he
> suddenly sees two rivers before him. The first river is a river
> of fire which lies to the south. The second river is a river of
> water which lies to the north. Each of these rivers is a hundred
> strides in width and has a depth which is unfathomable, and in
> length they are both unending to the north and south.
> A White Path lies between the rivers of fire and water. It is
> barely four or five inches wide. It stretches from the eastern
> bank to the western bank and is also a hundred strides long.
> The flames of the river of fire scorch the Path. The fire and
> water intermingle constantly and endlessly.
> Already this person has ventured far into a vast solitary
> clearing. There is no one there at all. In the distance are many
> bandits and vicious beasts. Seeing this person alone they vie
> with each other in their rush to kill him. Suddenly he finds
> himself (confronted with) the two great rivers. He thus thinks
> to himself (with alarm), 'These rivers have no borders to the
> south and north. The White Path between (these two rivers) is
> extremely narrow. Although the two banks are close, how can
> I possibly cross? Undoubtedly, I am going to die this very day.
> If I head back, then the bandits and vicious beasts will be
> closer. If I try to escape by fleeing to the south or north, the
> vicious beasts and poisonous insects will surely overtake me.
> If I try to cross the Path to the West, I will probably slip into
> either the river of water or the river of fire.' Whereupon
> unspeakable dread and fear fell upon him. Again he thought to
> himself, 'If I head back I am sure to die. If I stay, I am sure to
> die. If I proceed (along the White Path), I shall die. If there is
> no choice which enables me to escape death, then I would
> rather take my chances with the White Path and proceed
> ahead. This Path is before me and I must cross it without
> slipping.' At the very moment of his decision, he suddenly
> hears a voice on the eastern bank urging, 'All you have to do is

to decide to cross on this path. There is no danger of death. If you remain here, you are sure to die.' Then someone from the western bank calls saying, 'You, come at once with one mind and with right thought. I will protect you well. Do not fear falling into the dangers of fire and water.'

This person, having heard the persuasive voice and the imploring call from beyond, incorporates them in his body and mind. He then begins to cross the Path without fear or hesitation, and with no intention to turn back. After he has gone a step or two forward, the bandits on the eastern bank call out to him saying, 'You, come back. The Path is so dangerous that you will not be able to cross it. It is certain you will die. None of us wish you any harm.' Although this person hears the voices calling him he does not look back. With one mind, he promptly proceeds along the path. He is absorbed in treading it. In a short while he reaches the western bank. The various calamities are left behind forever and he meets the Good Friend. He rejoices greatly and unceasingly.[15]

Immediately following the parable in the text is Shan-tao's interpretation. The point Shan-tao emphasizes here is that in the midst of suffering man can become aware of something which trancends his mundane existence. In the parable this is the White Path which lies between the rivers of fire and water. Shan-tao interprets the White Path as "the capacity to give rise to the Pure Mind desiring rebirth in the Middle of greed and anger."[16]

The White Path became an essential feature of the landscape only when the man realized he was being pursued by bandits and vicious beasts. The parable gives the impression that the White Path has existed previously to this moment but has remained unnoticed by the man until his shadow motivated him to integrate these unconscious contents or be destroyed. In the parable it is apparent that ego-strength is most important. The endangered ego cannot in itself find the way out of the predicament, and thus it appears to be a hopeless situation in which even the choice to walk the White Path will lead to inevitable death. However, even the threatened ego has the final choice to make in determining the nature of its demise, rather its death will be a sacrifice or dissolution.

At the moment the man concedes his helplessness and chooses to proceed along the White Path, he hears the voices from the eastern and western banks encouraging and assuring him that he will not fall to his death. In the ego-sacrifice, the ego rearrangement of psychic conditions takes place, thus becoming aware of something supraordinate to itself. This awareness is the result of an expanded consciousness which was gained by the integration of the shadow with the assistance of the Self.

To the ego strengthened by integration of the unconscious contents, or the ego operating at a higher level of consciousness, the menacing power of the unconscious loses its destructiveness; thus, in the parable the bandits and vicious beasts suddenly appear friendly, and the fire and water covering the White Path are not harmful to the traveler.

Fire and water are natural opposites and mutually exclusive, yet they are united in covering the White Path. This is a parallel to an alchemical image of purification, or the process from the first stage of melanosis (blackening) to leukosis (whitening).[17] This is a process of awareness in which the energy invested in the unconscious has now broken up the original unconscious unity, and differentiation between black and white is taking place. Differentiation begins with getting in touch with the black or inferior and rejected side of one's own nature or the shadow, which Shan-tao understood as the part of the personality represented by the dangerous bandits and beasts as well as the rivers of fire and water, or greed and anger.

As we can see, in the ego-sacrifice the ego is not lost but has developed the ability to listen more to the self, and is strengthened and becomes flexible so that it is not overwhelmed by the contents of the unconscious. This is an example of ex-centric ego-consciousness, or creation of the ego/self axis. It is important not to confuse ego-sacrifice with ego-extermination or dissolution. In the ego-sacrifice the ego functions competently as the reality principle, but it is creatively responsive to the inner needs and is ready to work on the Taoistic principle of *wu-wei* or "let it happen." This strong and yet flexible attitude of the ego is externalized in the traveler's heeding of the advice given by the voice of Shakyamuni Buddha, urging the traveler to cross on the White Path.

Shan-tao uses the metaphor of the White Path to represent his teaching of *nien-fo*. With this choice of metaphor Shan-tao greatly deepens the practice of *nien-fo* because of the richness of associations with both the images of "white," and "path." A traditional Pure Land image of the pair of opposites "black and white" is that of white as the activity of the Buddha, or the genuine self, and black as man's efforts, or the ego's contrivance. Ego-centric calculations, or the blackening activity, can never be separated from the whitening activity of the self. Thus the whitening and blackening simultaneously occurs but Pure Land tradition holds that the whitening activity, or Buddha's karma, is much greater than man's black karma.

The image of the Path or bridge in Buddhist tradition is very important, touching the very heart of Buddhism. It is said that there are 84,000 *dharma* gates, or teachings, on the path of enlightenment. In a Chinese translation of the last sermon of the Buddha it is said that Buddha is "a dharma bridge to carry people over to the further port."[18] In the First Sermon of the Buddha he teaches the Enlightenment of the Middle Path consisting of the Noble Eightfold Way.[19] The two major traditions of Buddhism, Mahayana and Hinayana, contain the Sanskrit term *yana* which means the vehicle or path to enlightenment. The White Path of four or five inches is very narrow and yet it is called *tao*, or the Great Path, because it is the Buddha's path, and is wide enough for any man to walk in safety.

Walking the White Path of one hundred steps represents the total of man's life, thus indicating that the walker on the path, or the *nien-fo* practitioner, is involved in a lifelong endeavor to integrate unconscious contents by realizing the genuine self. The incessant contamination of fire and water, or anger and greed, must be continually transformed into wider consciousness if one is to live the symbolic life.

The voice of the self who calls saying "You, come at once with one mind and with right thought. . ." also represents the practice of *nien-fo*. In this practice of recitation, the ego's response to the Buddha's vow is indispensable, just as the response of the "you" addressed by the voice of the self, or the Buddha, is crucial. This situation is clearly reflected in one of the dreams that Shan-tao records after he finished writing his commentary. The dream goes as follows:

> There were three stone grain mortars revolving by themselves by the side of the road. Suddenly a person riding on a white camel appeared and encouraged me saying, 'Strive and make an effort and you will certainly be born into the Pure Land. Do not be lazy. Do not give up. This world is filled with filth and evil and much suffering. Do not be grief stricken, greedy or attached to the world.' I replied, 'I am most grateful for your wise instructions. Until the end of my life I will not dare to be lazy or greedy.[20]

In this dream Shan-tao positively responds to the admonishing person riding on the white camel thus demonstrating the importance of ego activity in relationship to the self in this tradition.

Contrary to the somewhat widespread impression that Asian religions aim at the dissolution of the ego, ego-strengthening is the goal of the Pure Land Buddhist practice of *nien-fo*. Through the creation of ex-centric ego-consciousness, or the activation of the ego/self axis, the ego dispels its erroneous identity with psycho-physical realities as taught in the doctrine of anatman. Shan-tao's parable of the White Path metaphorically relates the importance of *nien-fo* practice as a life-long endeavor that results in continual enrichment and widening of ego-consciousness.

FOOTNOTES

1. J. Jacobi, *The Way of Individuation*, trans. R.F.C. Hull (New York: Harcourt, Brace & World, Inc., 1967), p. 72.

J. Henderson, *The Jungian Orientation to Eastern Religion* - Lecture on a cassette tape (Los Angeles: C.G. Jung Institue, 1975).

2. Mokusen Miyuki, *The Secret of the Golden Flower, Studies and Translation*, Diploma Thesis for C.G. Jung Institute, Zurich. A German translation is published in *Kreisen des Lichtes: Die Erfahrung der Goldenen Blute* (West Germany: Otto Wilhelm Verlag, Weilheim/OBB, 1972), p. 248.

3. *Wu-liang-shou ching, Taisho* 12, No. 360. For a detailed account in English see *The Larger Sukhavati-vyuha* in F.M. Muller, ed., *Buddhist Mahayana Sutras* (*The Sacred books of the East*, Vol. XLIX (London: Oxford University Press, 1894).

4. The writer's translation from *Wu-liang-shou ching, Taisho* 12, No. 360, p. 258a. See also "Note" Ny Bunyin Nanjo in *The Larger Sukhavati-vyuha*, p. 73.

5. *Kuan Wu-liang-shou-fo ching Taisho* 37, No. 1753, p. 272b.

6. *Ibid.*, p. 272b.

7. *Ibid.*, p. 278b.

8. *Ibid.*, p. 278 b-c.

9. *Ibid.*, p. 278c.

10. C.G. Jung, "Psychology and Religion," *Psychology & Religion: West and East. The Collected Works of C.G. Jung* (hereafter abridged as CW), Vol. 11, p. 549.

11. C.G. Jung, "Foreward to 'Introduction to Zen Buddhism'," *CW*, Vol. 11, p. 549.

12. See, for instance, Ninian Smart, *The Religous Experience of Mankind* (New York: Charles Scribner's Sons, 1969), p. 90; Huston Smith, *The Religions of Man* (New York: Harper & Row, 1958), p. 127; H.C. Warren, *Buddhism in Translation* (New York: Atheneum Press, 1963), p. xiv, etc.

13. The Second Sermon of the Buddha is found in the *Mahavagga* and also in *The Samyutta-nikaya* III 66. For an English translation see E.J. Thomas, *The Life of Buddha* (New York: Barnes and Noble Inc., 1960), pp. 88-89.

14. C.G. Jung, "The Psychology of Eastern Meditation," *CW* Vol. II, p. 568.

15. *Kuan Wu-liang-shou-fo ching Taisho* 37, pp. 272c-273a.

16. *Ibid.*, pp.273 a-c.

17. C.G. Jung, *Psychology and Alchemy, CW* Vol. 12, p. 218.

18. *Yu hsing ching, Taisho* 1, No. 11.

19. *The Samyutta-nikaya* Vol. 420. For an English translation see E.J. Thomas, *Early Buddhist Scriptures* (London: Kegan Paul, Trench, Trubner & Co., LTD. 1935), pp. 29-33.

20. *Kuan Wu-liang-shou-fo ching Taisho* 37, p. 278c.

DYING ISAGI—YOKU

By Mokusen Miyuki

I became aware of the uniqueness of the Japanese attitude toward death when I participated in a workshop at the "Art of Dying" conference in 1974. This realization led me to further consideration of the Japanese perception of death and dying because it seems so different from common Western attitudes.

The Japanese response to the fear of death can be characterized as the attitude of *isagi-yoku*, a very important part of Japanese life. Dying *isagi-yoku* means to die with dignity and self-control. Such a death is considered to be the result of one's lifelong endeavor to face any emotional crisis with calmness and self-discipline.

In the East, death or dying is regarded as one's last enterprise in life; death exists inside or as a part of life, not outside of life or as the negation of life as in the West. Thus, in death the Easterner is concerned with inner attitude, or readiness to confront the horror of death, and in conducting oneself well in these last moments of life.

The reality of death and dying is integrated into one's effort to live meaningfully for the Japanese. The traditional Japanese feeling about life is that it is a journey and that each stage of this journey is equally important. Thus one "dies" at the end of each of the critical stages of life. In this tradition, aging is regarded not only as physical change but also as moral and spiritual growth.

Death is a concept. Dying, but not death, belongs to the experience of the living person. However, dying as a form of living is crucially different from other forms of living in that the individual is facing the critical moment in which he or she is going to disappear from this life. Here I present the Japanese response to the fear of death which can be characterized as the attitude of *isagi-yoku*.

Speaking of this attitude, D.T. Suzuki in his work *Zen and Japanese Culture* (1970) states:

> To die *isagi-yoku* is one of the thoughts very dear to the Japanese heart....*Isagi-yoku* means "leaving no regrets," "with a clear conscience," "like a brave man," "with no reluctance," "in full possession of mind," and so on. The Japanese hate to see death met irresolutely and lingeringly; they desire to be blown away like the cherry blossom before the wind, and no doubt this Japanese attitude toward death must have gone very well with the teachings of Zen (pp. 84-85).

Recently a friend of mine died. He was a *nisei* of about sixty who had cancer of the liver, and when I last visited him after he returned from the hospital, he appeared rather healthy in spite of the fact that he was expected to die within a few months. He knew he was approaching death, and I found I could offer him no words of consolation. When we shook hands he said to me, "I am ready to go." He survived long beyond the time expected by the doctors and his family, and during these last months he went many places and really seemed to enjoy his life. On the other hand, throughout these last months his life centered around the preparation for his death; he very carefully kept his personal belongings in order, bought a cemetery plot, made a will, and even washed the bowls from which he ate after every meal, thus indicating that he was quite ready to "leave" at every moment of his life. Nevertheless, according to his wife, from time to time he uttered the question, "Where am I going?" In fact, this was one of the last things he said.

I have a definite feeling that my friend knew that his question could only be answered by "going," or by experiencing death. He was driven to find the answer to his question by preparing to "leave" every moment, by living with his entire being from moment to moment. This man's words "Where am I going" were not uttered out of anguish or desperation. His careful preparations and calm acceptance of his fate were very possibly the reasons why he lived much longer than was expected.

This friend's experience suggests to me that, no matter how calmly or *isagi-yoku* one accepts death on the rational level, the total acceptance of death remains impossible on the existential level. There is a famous story about a Zen monk that makes this point: On his death bed a Zen master was asked by his disciples to leave his last words for them, and thus they brought him a brush and ink. The dying monk wrote, "I don't want to die. I don't want to die (*Shini tomo nai. Shini tomo nai*)." The disciples were very much perplexed and annoyed because the words did not seem to be those of an eminent Zen monk, so they asked him to write what he really felt. The monk then wrote, "Really, really (*Honmani, honmani*) [Kaneko, 1965]."

This story may conflict with our image of a great Zen master; the Zen monk is expected to be calm in facing death as the result of his *Zazen* practice which presumably enables him to live constantly in the here and now and to transcend the dichotomy of life and death. Assuredly this monk did not betray the general expectation as he wrote his last words with such self-composure, not in confusion and despair. The master was experiencing his immediate reality, which was his natural unwillingness to die, while in contrast his disciples were concerned with their image of what it means to be a famous Zen master. As with the experience of my friend, this story seems to convey that, as long as we live, the natural attachment to our physical existence is undeniable, even for someone who has cultivated the ability to transcend life and death.

In this connection I am reminded of Kishimoto Hideo, a Japanese scholar in the field of religion. He suffered for many years from a terminal illness and left us a valuable document which contains his talks about his experience of death in life, and also a manuscript in which he set down his perception of what it means to die. Being driven by the physical terror of death, which he characterized as incomprehensible, unquenchable "thirst or hunger for life," he had hopelessly attempted to intellectualize about the life hereafter. As he was a scholar, he first endeavored, in vain, to convince himself to accept his fate by utilizing the religious knowledge which he had accumulated. As in our previous stories, the attachment to physical life was unquestionably overwhelming for him. Then, he writes (Kishimoto, Kamei, Karaki, & Shimoyama, 1964), suddenly one day he had a flash of illumination:

> The only necessary thing is our preparation to confront death when it comes. . .What I discovered here was that I was afraid of death because I was thinking that I would experience it, and then I discovered that death was outside of my experience.

What we can experience is only life or living. It was a shocking experience for me to realize that there is no other way permitted for human beings to live except to keep living [p. 61].

Kishimoto (1962) goes on to state that death is simply the lack of life, and the only thing given to us is life or living, nothing else. Thus his question became very clear. "How can I 'really' live what is left of my life?" Since life, for which he was "thirsty," was no more granted, he tried to live best each and every given moment beyond which there was no further assurance of life. He convinced himself that it was necessary for him to be ready to confront death at any moment when it came with the attitude of calmly bidding farewell to his life. Thus, whenever he said goodbye to others, he experienced that moment as if it had been the last opportunity for him to exchange these words.

Russel Noyes, Jr., (1973) who has written several articles on death, calls attention to the stoic philosopher Seneca's view that one must prepare for death each day if one is to die happily. According to Kishimoto, this attitude was the only way he could face the physical fear of death and best live his given life. Like Seneca, Kishimoto submitted himself to the necessity of death and demonstrated the freedom of the human will in choosing his attitude in confronting death. As McKissack (1974) has suggested, fear of death can provide the impetus for further growth. Thus Kishimoto's efforts to live consciously and fully in the present began as soon as he was sentenced to death by his terminal illness, and his stance of constantly dying to his previous self seems to have enabled him to exist in the immediate present (see Eigen, 1974).

Kishimoto's attitude of being ready to confront death with a calm and serene mind, as the result of his effort to experience each and every moment of living as the last moment, reminds me of the story about the famous *haiku* poet Basho (Iwami, 1958). Basho (1643-1694) when he was about to die at the age of fifty-one, composed a *haiku* which can be translated:

> In my journey
> I suffer from sickness.
> And yet my dreams
> Are running in the withered fields [p.44].

Basho's disciples asked him: "Can we consider this *haiku* as the last one that you leave to us?" He answered, "this *haiku* that I composed throughout my life is no other than my last [p. 46]."

Thus, Basho referred to his attitude or way of living in the presence of death. Basho was not a hermit nor did he abhor life; rather, he loved his life deeply, and all the more so by living his life in the presence of death. With the conviction that one travels through life as if it were a journey, one becomes aware that each and every stage of the journey is the ultimate in itself and should be lived with one's entire being and effort in the expectation of death.

In the eyes of the man with this conviction, the world he lives in appears at each and every moment as extremely beautiful and as the manifestation of eternal life itself. Like the following poem translated by Suzuki (1970).

> **Of an approaching death**
> **Showing no signs**
> **The cicada's droning [p.252].**

Such a short lived insect that puts all of its efforts in singing in harmony with the forest intrigued the mind of the poet. As a nature poet, Basho does not speak of the cicada as outside of himself but as his inner reality through which he experiences the approach of death. Suzuki has commented on this poem saying: "The cicada is perfect, content with itself and with the world. . .As long as it can sing it is alive, and while alive there is an eternal life and what is the use of worrying about transitoriness [p. 252]"? In hearing the cicada's drone perhaps Kishimoto would have felt that even the cicada was saying goodbye to its life by living each moment with great intensity, or, while "showing no signs" of approaching death.

The question then arises, why was it so desirable for Kishimoto and the poet Basho to have a calm mind, undisturbed by the fear of death? To find an answer to this question, we must consider the Japanese cultural tradition. According to Kishimoto, the place occupied by death in the East and West differs because of the socio-cultural traditions involved. In the West, death is outside of life as well as the negation of life, and people tend to make an issue of whether or not the dying person physically suffered. In the East, death or dying is regarded as one's last enterprise in life; death exists inside, or as a part of the journey of life. The concern is therefore not with physical pain or suffering, as in the West, but rather with the kind of attitude the person had when he or she met death. What is the most important for the Easterner is the demonstration of control over the fear of death, and this control is considered to be the result of a lifelong effort to keep the mind calm and serene in the face of any emotional experiences. "If a person died in despair feeling deserted by his God as in the case of Christ, it could never be considered a good death in the East (Kishimoto & Mansutani, 1955)." It would seem that Kishimoto understands Christ as being filled with agony at the time of his death and in the East this would not be an appropriate death for one who is spiritually matured. For the Easterner, the idea of a good death is exemplified by the description of the death of Buddha, found in the *Maha-parimibhana Suttanta*. Buddha passed away while experiencing *samadhi*, or the calmness and peacefulness of mind, which was the result of his lifelong meditation practice (see Rhys-Davids, 1969, pp. 114-116). Also, the account of the deaths of the great Zen masters who passed away in Zen meditation, as a result of the virtue of their life's efforts, is greatly admired by the Japanese (Miyuki, 1976 p. 258). Thus, in death the Easterner is concerned with inner attitude, or readiness to confront the horror of death, and in conducting oneself well in these last moments of life.

The Japanese would appreciate Montaigne (1948) who maintained, "He who would teach men to die would teach them to live [p.62]." Being able to meet death in an admirable manner is considered to be the result of one's lifelong endeavor and discipline. Self-discipline, or mind cultivation (*kokoro no shuyo*), in order to achieve tranquility, calmness, and impartiality, is developed in many ways for the Japanese. Religion, morality, and art are all interrelated in Japanese culture and all aim at producing the desired mind quality. D.T. Suzuki's (1970) work has made many Westerners aware of the close relationship of Zen and art, Japanese religion, and artistic activities in general. This interrelationship is seen in the fact that anyone and everyone can be artistic in the Japanese cultural tradition. Consequently, there is no special class of artists in traditional Japan, and the Japanese tend to want to make their lives as artistic or aesthetic as possible. Thus to be artistic for the Japanese is not separated from aesthetic living and cultivation of a calm mind which enables one to have distance when facing an emotional crisis. From this viewpoint we can also understand why the Japanese emphasize the importance of one's inner state when facing death.

The emphasis on the discipline of self-control in the face of death is carried to excess. The Japanese tend to judge a dead person's integrity on the basis of externally observed facts. As a matter of fact, the bereaved family, and especially, the wife, of my friend who passed away saying "where am I going," felt somewhat unhappy regarding the man's peace of mind. However, when I told them the story of the Zen master who wrote, "I don't want to die" on his deathbed, they felt very much relieved, for they thought that if even the self-disciplined Zen master did not want to accept the reality of death, then how much more so this must have been with their beloved one.

I had another experience in this regard when about a year ago an elderly lady died. She was a very gentle and agreeable person but she had no children and led a lonesome life. As she grew older, she showed an astounding attachment to material things; it was as though material things were the only source of security for her. Those Japanese who attended her funeral service, regardless of their age or religion, spoke to each other about how tense her death mask was, and that it was as if she showed in it an incurable, unshakable attachment to the material wealth that she left behind. It is quite understandable that this lady's horror of death on the physical level might well have resulted in her tense death mask. Nevertheless, the Japanese believe that the facial expression at death is not the result of physical pain but reflects the interior quality of the person. Thus, it seems commonly held that if we want to show a beautiful face when we die, we have to prepare an attitude of detachment which is characterized as *isagi-yoku*. Dying *isagi-yoku* is the attitude of being ready to face death in such a manner that neither we nor others have regrets. However, as I will discuss later, this attitude is also used in reference to any other critical moment of life.

The attitude that life should be like the flower blossoms on the trees that fall to the ground was embodied in the archetypal image that gripped the Kamikaze pilots in World War II. A common expression in the Japanese language is "to make the flower of death bloom (*shini-bana o sakaseru*)," and in the minds of the Kamikaze warriors this archetype of death must have been activated and played an important role in giving meaning to their lives. Another example of this attitude is found in the medieval era in Japan when warriors went into battle, after being purified and wearing their best clothes and armour, made up so that they could die as beautifully as possible.

This aesthetic attitude toward death should not be confused with a romantic conception of life or living outside of reality. In this sense dying *isagi-yoku* is always concerned with the concrete reality of life. The Japanese extend the idea of dying *isagi-yoku* not only to the physical act of dying but also to symbolic "acts of dying" which occur at each and every important stage of life in which one experiences an emotional crisis. Marriage, separation from loved ones, retirement, or resignation are all transitions in life, the Japanese want to encounter them with detachment, calmness, and tranquility. Thus, for the Japanese one should take the initiative in matters of the inevitable: Retiring under the age limit, or retiring from the stage, or a farewell *sumo* match, are all regarded as demonstration of one's integrity in terms of dying *isagi-yoku*. As Rohlen (1976) has observed, this attitude toward aging is the embodiment of Confucian ideals in which aging implies not only physical changes by moral and spiritual growth. Accordingly, the reality of death and dying for the Japanese is integrated into one's effort to live meaningfully.

REFERENCES

Eigen, M. Fear of death: A symptom with changing meanings. *Journal of Humanistic Psychology*, 1974, **14** (3), 29-33.

Iwami, M. *Nihon geido to Bukkyo no Kokoro* (The Japanese Arts and Buddhism). Kyoto: Nagata bunshodo, 1958.

Kaneko, D. *Shi o Kaky Kanzu* (My view of Death). *Zaike Bukkyo*, 1965, **119**, 29-30.

Kishimoto, H. *Hitotsu no Senkoku* (A Final Sentence). *Zaike Bukkyo*, 1962 **100**. 52-57

Kishimoto, H., Kamei, S., Karaki, J., & Shimoyama, T. *Nihonjin no Shiseikan* (The Japanese View of Death and Life). *Zaike Bukkyo*, 1964, **117**, 46-63.

Kishimoto, H., & Mansutani, B. *Toyo to Seiyo* (East and West). *Zaike Bukkyo*, 1955, **20**, 8-14.

Miyuki, M. Chinese response to Buddhism: The case of Hua-yen Tsung. In L. Thompson (ed.), *Studia Asiatica*. Taipei & San Francisco: Chinese Center Press, 1976.

Montaigne, M. In Donald M. Frame (trans.), *The complete works of Montaigne*. Vol I Stanford Calif.: Stanford University Press, 1948.

Noyes, R. Seneca on death. *Journal of Religion and Health*. 1973, **12** (3), 223-240.

Rhys-Davids, T.W. The Maha-parimibhana Suttanta. *Buddhist Sutras*. New York: Dover Publications, 1969.

Rohlen, T. The promise of adulthood in Japanese spiritualism. *Daedalus*, 1976, **105** (2), 125-143.

Suzuki, D. *Zen and Japanese culture* (4th ed.) Princeton: Princeton University Press, 1970.

THE PSYCHODYNAMICS
OF BUDDHIST MEDITATION
A Jungian Perspective
By Mokusen Miyuki

Both Jungian and Buddhist meditation are concerned with the man who experiences a feeling of disorientation. Their aim is to help the suffering man restore his balance, and in this sense they are both related to personal experience.

In this age of dehumanization, restoration of the alienated part of ourselves, which is both highly personal and unique, is extremely important for our well-being. We tend to consider personal experience as subjective, in the sense that it is idiosyncratic; thus, we surmise that no one is able to thoroughly understand another's experience. It seems to me, however, that the most personal experiences are those which are most universal. Imagine you are walking down a path on a very dark night. Suddenly you see a snake crawling toward you. You are so frightened that you feel you may have a heart attack. Careful observation, however, reveals that it is a rope in front of you, not a snake. We could regard this kind of experience as both idiosyncratic and pathological, the result of a personal illusion; yet many people have experiences of this nature, which we can understand psychologically as a projection[1] of inner fear onto an external reality. In this sense, what takes place in such a situation is part of the common human experience.

Also, in this connection, consider the love stories in world literature; each is culturally conditioned besides being individually different, and yet they all have a universal quality to them. This may sound superfluous, but each of us who loves someone feels that there is only one such occurrence of this particular kind in past, present, or future. However, this feeling of love, as well as what we do about it, is very personal and at the same time universal. Consequently, I hope that my discussion, which aims at communicating what I consider to be the essentials of my experience in Jungian analysis and Buddhist meditation, will have a universal dimension.

From time to time, I have conducted analysis in conjunction with *zazan*. One such case involved a friend of mine, a professional man, who was forty-eight years old. A few years before, his marriage got into trouble. When he came to see me, he was very depressed and had suicidal tendencies. This man was born into a prestigious family in Japan and received a good education. His wife was several years older than he and they had no children. I asked him to come whenever he wanted to and for the first ten days he came every other day. Since he was a Judo expert, I suggested to him that we Sit together.[2] Sometimes he stayed more than three hours, relating his past experiences and his understanding and feelings about his life. He said he felt very much relieved to be Sitting with me.

Ten days later he brought a dream to discuss. Since he had no dreams for many years, he was really surprised to have had such a clear one. The dream goes as follows: "I was walking along in an unknown desert. There were around me many big horse-like animals, all dead. I felt sick but I also felt that I must go my way."

In contrast to Freud, who considered dreams a distorted fulfillment of repressed wishes, both sexual and moral, Jung regards dreams as spontaneous portrayals of the actual situation of the unconscious in symbolic language; that is, they are a natural expression of the unconscious process.[3] Unlike Freud, who tried to interpret dreams to get at the latent content of the manifested material, Jung accepted the dream context as presented. He regarded the dream as an experience, not unlike daily life. Hence, he maintains that the dream is meaningful on its own: it should not be tied to judgement and evaluation by the ego-centered consciousness.

What, then, is the significance of dreams to the individual according to Jung? For him, life is a process that flows between the poles of consciousness and the unconscious. Thus, he maintains the hypothesis that dreams, or other materials from the unconscious, e.g., visions fantasies, are to be understood, or appreciated, in conjunction with the conscious situation. This can be best visualized by using the Chinese symbolism of *T'ai Chi*, or the Great Ultimate, as the dynamic totality of the interplay of the opposites of *yin-yang*, with *yin* as the unconscious and *yang* as consciousness. This technically implies, in the case of dream analysis, that we must ask what kind of associations the dreamer has regarding the images in the dream.

I asked my friend what associations he had to his dream. The only association he gave me was that the dead animals, perhaps horses, reminded him of his wife because she was born in the year of the horse. He was unable to say anything else since he was so depressed. He told me, however, that he strongly felt the importance of "the act of going on his own way." I also stressed the importance of his decision to choose his own way although the destination was unknown: his way might mean self-destruction and he should be prepared to accept this possiblity.

Since the man's most urgent problem was with getting a divorce, and recovering his lost life energy, he pessimistically regarded himself as condemned by the entire Japanese community. Japanese of his age generally regard marriage as an almost sacred institution, not between two loving hearts but between two families. To want to divorce his wife evoked a perception of himself as hopeless and unworthy. He was unable to accept himself as a divorced person.

If you look at the dream from the man's situation, it compensates for his conscious attitude. It says: you must realize you have chosen your own way even though you feel lost; even though you cannot decide to do anything; everything else is barren and dead, and yet you are ready to go your own way. Jung maintains that the dream can function as a compensation to the conscious situation of the dreamer. Consequently, without having the associations of the dreamer we cannot make a personal interpretation of it. These associations are often confessional and very painful; in the case of my friend, even to say that he wanted to divorce his wife was very hard. Compared to his "ideal" self-image, getting a divorce was for him hopelessly devastating and too painful to accept.

The part of our being which we neglect and find inferior to our conscious image of ourselves is designated by Jung as the shadow. Nevertheless, unless we accept the shadow part of ourselves, we cannot be a total being. By being aware of this dark side, one enlarges and strengthens consciousness. This confrontation of consciousness with the unconscious, brings forth contents which, when integrated, leads to what Jung has called the transcendent function. What emerges is transcendent to both. Jung defines the transcendent function as "the way of obtaining liberation by one's own effort and by finding the courage to be oneself."[4]

Since my friend had no other associations, I asked him to use his dream as a way to experience himself, or as a *koan*, in conjunction with his Sitting. A *koan* is enigmatic for the rational intellect. What is expressed in the *koan* is *satori* -- an experience of the numinous. The individual who has undergone *satori* feels a change of attitude towards life. The *koan* conveys this highly personal and original event. "What is your original face and eye" is a famous *koan* revealing the *satori* experience.[5] The Zen master Lin-chi (Japanese, Rinzài Gigen, d. 866) also expressed his *satori* as the realization of the "True man of no rank" appearing within and without through one's breathing in and out.[6] Unmistakably, both the "original face and eye" and the "true man of no rank" refer to the unique ground of our being, or our genuine personal identity. This is personal, and at the same time, universal.

Zen often speaks metaphorically of the experience of this real self as "getting through the bottom of one's being." The water in a bucket which is placed in the ocean, merges into it if the bottom of the bucket is removed. One and the same water is then found both inside and outside of the bucket; thus, the reality of the water is one. The Buddhist teaching of *anatman*, or non-substantiality, is based on this experience of the unity of life, or the oneness of water within and without the bucket. *Anatman* is not a metaphysical but a psychological statement, in the sense that it is an expression of the awareness of this bottomless ground of one's existence or the unity of life. Zen, therefore, has an optimistic as well as a stubborn faith in one's real self as being both personal and universal.

This fundamental faith in oneself found in Zen is articulated by Lin-chi as faith not in supernatural beings but in one's own being.[7] The practice of Zen sitting is carried out, based on this faith. The real self thusly fulfills itself, the forgetting of one's boundaries of individual existence takes place, and the cosmic reality of the Buddha as *dharma-kaya* (the body of truth) manifests itself. To quote Dogen (1200-1253), the founder of the Soto school of Zen in Japan, "To learn Buddha Dharma is to learn oneself. To learn oneself is to forget oneself. To forget oneself is to be experienced in the myriad of things."[8] Elsewhere, Dogen also appreciates his experience of the bottomless self as the activity of the Buddha:

> Being single-minded, you throw your body and mind into the house of the Buddha and forget them. Being thusly carried on by the hand of the Buddha, you follow the activity of the

Buddha and you are free from the life and death (of *samsara*) to become the Buddha, without effort and without exerting your mind.[9]

It is important to point out that the term "Buddha" simply means "the awakened one." Awareness of oneself has been very much stressed in Buddhist tradition. However, gaining self-knowledge never ceases as long as we live. In this sense, we can say that the "self" can only be defined by the act of walking the path of our life, or, is "to be experienced in the myriad of things." Since no human being lives in a vacuum, the act of walking is understood in relation to one's environment, just as the water in the bucket forms a continuum with the water outside of it. The action of one is that of the other and the existence of the two is a continuous process which is interdependent, reciprocal, and transactive. It forms a field of patterns of countless relationships consisting of numerous sequences of connected events. As discussed above, Zen has a fundamental faith in the inner man as being original, spontaneous, creative, free and unique. Therefore, this field of functional relationships of the individual and his environment is to be understood as a creative process of the entire universe.

Psychologically speaking, by focusing on a *koan* one can create a vacuity in consciousness.[10] Thus, consciousness is wide open to the emergence of new contents from the unconscious. This results in an altered state. This experience, in my opinion, is referred to in Buddhist tradition as Interdependent Origination. The simplest formulation of this teaching, which is found in many canons, is as follows:

When this is, that is;
This arising, that arises;
When this is not, that is not;
This ceasing, that ceases.[11]

Since "this" and "that" symbolized all possible opposites, to experience both "this" and "that" as they are is to experience them as part of the dynamic whole of Interdependent Origination and psychologically speaking can be considered as the transcendent function. Zen Sitting can, therefore, be understood as a form of the transcendent function as it facilitates the transition from one psychological condition to another by the mutual confrontation of opposites, namely "this" as consciousness and "that" as the unconscious.

I asked my friend to express whatever feelings, images, or ideas that occurred to him during Sitting so that he could integrate "that", or the unconscious part of his being, into "this" or his conscious sphere. In this way, I expected him to become aware of the other half of himself which he despised so much. I hoped that the growing awareness of "that," would gradually compensate the menacing power of "this," or his conscious perception of himself as so hopelessly lost and suicidal.

My friend seemed to have gained a new perspective on his life. Clearly, his existence cannot be separated from the way he poses the question, "where am I going, or why am I going?" This is not mentioned in his dream at all. Why is simply "going his way" emphasized? What conscious situation, then, is compensated for by this act of going? I had a feeling that he did not want to go on with his life; he was afraid that he was ready to commit suicide and this was also very much feared by his wife. In this sense, for him, where to and what for were not the issues, but simply going on was the point. Life is an on-going process, here and now. Pursuit of what should be makes us blind to what is. We should be aware of the value of our own existence in terms of simply being. This creative receptiveness and responsiveness to what-is, is the message from the dream to compensate this man's suicidal impulse.

The dead horses which my friend associated with his wife were also a major symbol in this dream. This man seems to be a sensualist and thus his wife was represented as an animal, indicating that he related himself to her instinctively. In other words, his image of femininity, or women, was on the level of instinct, not on the level of human subtlety. It is vitally necessary for this person to develop his image of women; to differentiate it, to appreciate it, and to articulate the feeling of life contained therein. Obviously, he does not need a dead animal, and yet it is part of him. What is dead in this dream is not outside of him but inside; namely, the feeling of life connected to his wife to whom he related instinctively.

According to Jung, the image of woman in the male is termed the *anima*. The *anima* is personified normally as a contra-sexual figure in the dreams. On the other hand, the *animus* is the masculine nature of women and is also usually personified in woman's dreams as male. It is generally maintained by Jung that one has to deal with his shadow before he can deal with the *anima* or the *animus*, simply because the latter two are more archaic, in the sense of being less differentiated than the shadow, and would thus appear very dangerous, nonsensical, and unpredictable. This man's dream indicates that his shadow is projected on the image of walking alone, whereas his *anima* is projected onto the dead horse and is not up to the level of a human being. This shows that his capacity to perceive and relate to the feminine is lacking.

Dreams are also related to collective or objective ideas and, in this vein, I would like to take up the symbol of the horse in this dream. According to Japanese astrology, the woman born in the fire-horse year (*hinoeuma*) is sometimes considered as a man-eater. Often that kind of woman has a difficult time finding a husband, even today. My friend mentioned that his wife was speaking of her life with him after retirement. He felt, however, that he could not accept that kind of feeling and attitude about life. He really felt that his future was dead as far as his life with her was concerned. One could say that he did not want to be eaten up by his "horse wife." With this consideration of the collective Japanese image regarding "horse women," we are amplifying the dream image of horses, not only on a subjective level but also on the collective level. This method uses symbols found in world literature, myths, fairy tales, religions, astrology, etc., to amplify dream images.[12]

When we focus on the "act of going," besides its function of compensating this man's feeling of being so lost as to consider suicide, we get a universal image of human existence. One's own way is clearly personal, belonging to each and every individual, and yet the act of going on one's way is quite universal. One cannot go anywhere except by finding where one is in the here and now. "Going," therefore, is dependent upon "being here", and "becoming" is an expression of being oneself. This paradoxical image that "becoming is being" is understood as an image of what Jung calls the Self. The Self has a very paradoxical nature, being simultaneously the center and the circumference of the psyche, as well as the core of one's existence. If you ask who is the author of this dream, which is a very pertinent question for this man's critical situation, the answer given by Jung would be that it is the Self. The Self is not only the author of the dream but is expressed by it. If we consider my friend's dream from such a perspective, we find it neither subjective nor objective, but micro-macro cosmic. The foregoing would be considered an analysis on the level of the Self, or individuation.

In my understanding, many Zen *koans* can be understood as the expression of the psychological process termed "individuation." My friend's dream reveals many levels; which level is most needed or important for his awareness cannot be decided until we know his associations. On the level of the Self, however, the dream can function as a Zen *koan*. The meaning of a *koan* is never explicit, because our awareness is limited by many personal factors such as our interests, education, background, or our suffering and joy. Furthermore, Zen *koans* are individual and related to the personal events in the life of Zen practitioners in their critical moment of *satori*. The only way in which they can be "understood" is through serious involvement in Zen practice.

Jung uses the term individuation "to denote the process by which a person becomes a psychological 'in-dividual' that is, a separate, indivisible unity or whole."[13] Jung discovered, in his many years of clinical experience and practice, that the process of becoming oneself is unique to the individual and depends on one's psychological condition at any given time. The individuation process, which involves integration of conscious and unconscious, gives a sense of purpose, or meaning, to life which makes the individual a unique person. In connection with my friend's case, walking the path alone does not refer to any concrete or objective end, and yet he himself cannot experience himself as an individual unless he walks that path. Herein, one finds a very important idea in Jungian psychology which is termed finality; this term refers to "immanent psychological striving for a goal," or for "a sense of purpose."[14] With this concept of finality, Jung differentiates analytical psychology from Freudian psychoanalysis and Adlerian individual psychology. As is well known, Freud introduced the idea of causality in understanding neurosis as being determined by past traumas, while Adler's perspective of neurosis was that it was a product of the will to power emanating from one's inferiority complex.

Both Freud and Adler consider the human psyche from a deterministic point of view. In contrast to this psychological determinism, Jung's viewpoint is "finalistic" *(telos)*. It recognizes causality of both the past and the future, but its emphasis is upon those phenomena demonstrating "immanent psychological striving for a goal," thus respecting spontaneity, creativity, and freedom in the individual psyche.

In order to be an individual, my friend had to walk alone on his path. Here we need to ask the question again, but this time in a different context: what is dead in this dream? We pointed out that if we regard this man's dream from a subjective level of interpretation, his relationship and feeling towards his wife was dead. However, I was curious about the intensity of his anger and his strong condemnation of his wife. As I discussed above, he insisted that his wife was depriving him of the possiblity of realizing himself by always talking about their retirement. A protest of such strength, and the fact that he repeated it so often, made me suspicious. He gradually came to realize that the other side of this anger and condemnation was connected with his childish reliance on his wife. I also felt his anger was directed towards himself because he was so dependent on his mother-wife that he was incapable of going his way alone. Viewed in this manner, the dream death of the "horse wife" also represents the death of this man's morbid dependence. As a matter of fact, his anger against his wife later turned into an appreciation of the nourishment and care he received from her over the past twenty years. Unless he could accept himself as dying to his old self, (the death of his morbid dependence) he could never be himself, or the in-divisible one. Paradoxically stated, dying is living for this man.

The theme of dying to one's old relationships and perceptions is often found in Zen *koans*. The one that comes to mind in this connection is Hyakujo's Fox.[15] I would like to paraphrase it: Whenever the Zen master Hyakujo (in Chinese Po-change, 720-814) delivered a sermon, a certain old man was always there listening to it with the other monks. However, one day the old man did not leave with the other monks but remained in the lecture hall so Hyakujo became curious and asked him who he was. The old man answered, "I am not a human being. In the past, namely in the time of the Kasho Buddha, I was a head monk, like you, here in this very same temple. One time a monk came to me and asked whether an enlightened one could fall into the *samsaric, karmic* existence. I answered 'No'. In this way, I fell into the state of being a fox and I have gone through five hundred lives as a fox. Now, I beg you to give me one word that will release me from this fox state." Thereupon he asked Hyakujo, "Does an enlightened man fall into the *samsaric, karmic* existence?" Hyakujo answered, "No, *karmic* law is evident." With that very utterance the old man was thoroughly enlightened. He said, "I am now released from the state of being a fox. My body will be found in the backyard of the temple. I dare make a request of you: please bury me according to the funeral customs for a monk." Hyakujo thus ordered the monk in charge to beat the clapper and inform the other monks to hold a funeral service after the midday meal. The monks thought this very strange because all of them were in good health and no one was in the infirmary. After the meal, Hyakujo led them to the base of a rock in the backyard. With his stick, he dug out the body of the fox and had it cremated. In the evening, Hyakujo went to the rostrum in the lecture hall and told the monks the whole story. Obaku (in Chinese, Huang-po, d. 850?), a disciple of Hyakujo, thereupon asked, "The old man made a mistake in his answer and fell into the state of a fox for five hundred lives, you say? But what would have happened to him if he made no mistake?" Hyakujo replied, "Just come up here near me and I'll tell you what would have happened."

Then Obaku went up to Hyakujo and boxed his ears. Hyakujo, clapping his hands and laughing, exclaimed, "I should say that the barbarian has a red beard, but here I should also say that there is a barbarian with a red beard."

This *koan* may sound extremely strange. In a relationship between master and disciple, how could the disciple box the ears of the master? Some scholars maintain that Zen is iconoclastic. Not only beating the masters, but even burning the sacred statue of the Buddha -- an incredibly blasphemous act for the religious consciousness -- has been noted in Zen history. However, when we ask, who is this old man who lived in the same place as our Zen master, Hyakujo? We then have a strong feeling that this old man, who was condemned to the fox state, must have been connected to Hyakujo sometime in the past. In Buddhist tradition, reincarnation of enlightened individuals is not an alien motif. As a matter of fact, in the *Jataka*, the Buddha himself is said to have reincarnated into countless beings before he became enlightened. During these lives he took many forms, both animal and human, in which he practiced his teaching of compassion. In this *koan*, Hyakujo is obviously referred to as the one who is ready to get into the *samsaric* existence of *karma* by his act of compassion. In this spirit, he must have "died to himself" numerous times, say five hundred or more. There is no end of compassion for Hyakujo in living his own way as an enlightened master.

Karma refers to one's existence. The term *karma* is derived from the verb *kr* which means to do, or to act. Thus *karma* means action of the individual. However, as I discussed before, the individual never lives in a vacuum and his action invites the reaction of others. This is then countered by his reaction to this reaction *ad infinitum*. Hence, *karma* not only refers to the personal dimension of the individual but also to the collective dimension of action/reaction encompassing the entire chain of life. Thus *karma* is also regarded as Inter-dependent Origination in the Buddhist tradition. In this sense, *karma* is one's own existence but this can never be separated from the process of action/reaction in the entire universe. No one can be free from his own *karma*. In Buddhism, however, the enlightened one is characterized as the one who transcends his *karmic* bondage. Hence, nothing is wrong with the fox-master's answer.

In this *koan*, the point, in my understanding, is the attitude towards one's own *karmic* existence. Conceiving of enlightenment as being free from *karma* is based on the perception of it as something external, whereby one is controlled by something outside of oneself. In this sense, there is no appreciation or acceptance of one's own being as spontaneous and creative: he is simply not himself. However, the monk Hyakujo's answer clearly shows his acceptance of his *karmic* existence. By his acceptance, he becomes a free and creative individual. The difference lies in one's attitude towards one's own *karma*. One is in *karma* and yet not bound by it if one accepts it. We often think that freedom is realized only when we can make ourselves free from bondage, which is usually conceived of as external constraint. We must realize, however, that bondage is also one's own perception or understanding of reality. Just like my friend, who died to his own perception of his wife, the Zen master Hyakujo must have experienced the death of his perception of himself as a free man as many as five hundred times. Transcending one's own *karma* and being enlightened is the unceasing process of becoming oneself. In this sense, being oneself can never be separated from "the way." This is expressed in Buddhism quite often. For instance, in the Chinese version of Buddha's last sermon, we read that Buddha is a ferryman. He crossed over to the far shore, both alone and taking others. Buddha is the *dharma* bridge. He is the great path or way which enables man to cross over the river of *samsara*.[16]

As Jung says, a *koan* is a means to create "an almost perfect lack of conscious assumptions."[17] This means that the withdrawal of the center of psychic gravity centered around the ego takes place and is followed by the creation of a new psychic condition that is not ego-centric but ex-centric, meaning that the center of consciousness is in a state of flux. In the ex-centric state of mind, one can experience a spontaneous interplay of images, visions, feelings and ideas which are partially related to past experience. Therefore, one can sense his present condition in various ways by integrating these contents, thus enlarging his awareness. In *zazen* (with a *koan*) what takes place is a rearrangement of psychic conditions which can result in the creation of a new identity or personality.

In the case of my friend, many associations regarding his past experiences centering around the "dead horse" were activated and related to me. In this manner, his psychic contents were rearranged and he was able to strenghten his consciousness. Thus, he activated a new attitude and feeling for life. This new personality of his, so to speak, was no longer defensive and rigid with fear. In this way, he was able to decide for himself to confront his wife. In reality, he confronted her, as I said before, not with the feeling of fear and condemnation, but with appreciation and hope for the emergence of new life.

In speaking of the application of Buddhist meditation to Jungian analysis, we must have a common ground. This common ground, in my experience, is one's attitude to life. In the case of Zen meditation, nothing external, even the dogmas or creeds of Buddhism, are sacrosanct. In the case of analysis, the issue is not theories of the human psyche but an attitude of honest commitment and the acceptance of one's worst self. If any change is to take place, one must die to the previous self. To do this presupposes an awareness and reintegration of one's alienated self. This has traditionally been spoken of in the famous Zen dictum *that whatever comes from without is not the genuine treasure of yourself.* Another famous statment that I mentioned before expresses this as "to realize one's original face and eye." To be an individual, in the Jungian sense of the individuation process, shares, in my opinion, many of the same underlying processes as found in Zen. I fully agree with Jung, therefore, when he says that Zen, "can be understood as an Eastern method of psychic healing, i.e. making whole."[18]

REFERENCES

1. "Projection means the expulsion of a subjective content into an object. . .Accordingly it is a process of dissimilation by which a subjective content becomes alienated from the subject and is, so to speak, embodied in the object. . .We may distinguish passive and active projection. The passive form is the customary form of all pathological and many normal projections; they are not intentional and are purely automatic occurrences." C.G. Jung, *The Collected Works of C.G. Jung* (hereafter referred to as *CW*), vol. 6 (Princeton, N.J.: Princeton University Press, 1971), pp. 457-458.

2. The principle of Judo is non-resistance which is based on the Buddhist teaching of *anatman* (Japanese *muga*), or being free from ego-calculation or ego-attachment. For a further discussion of Judo see the article "Judo and Psycho-physical Unity" by Robert Linssen in *The World of Zen*, edited by Nancy Wilson Ross (New York: Vintage Books, 1960), pp. 291-292.

3. For Jung's interpretation of dreams, see the following two articles: "The Nature of Dreams" and "General Aspects of Dream Psychology" in *CW*, vol. 8.

4. *Ibid.*, p. 91.

5. This famous Zen expression is traditionally ascribed to the Sixth Patriarch Huineng (638-713). See D.T. Suzuki, *Essays in Zen Buddhism: First Series* (London: Rider & Co., 1948, p. 211.

6. *Chen-chou Lin-chi Hui-chao Ch'an-shih Yu-lu* (The Dialogues of the Zen Master Lin-chi Hui-chao of Chen-chou), edited by Hui-jan. *Taisho Shinshu Daizokyo* (Taisho Edition of the Tripitaka in Chinese), edited by J. Takakusu, et al. (Tokyo: 1924-1934), vol. 47 no. 1984, p. 496c.

7. *Ibid.*, pp. 496b-c, 497b, 498a, 499b 501a, 501b, 502c, etc.

8. *Shobogenzo*, edited by Eto Sokuo, 3 vols. (Tokyo: Iwanami Shoten, 15th printing, 1964), vol. 1. pp. 83-84.

9. *Ibid.*, vol. #, p.240.

10. The Chinese term "Ch'an," or Zen in Japanese, is a transliteration of the Pali "jhana," or Sanskrit "dhyana", which is often used synonymously with "samadhi" in the Buddhist tradition. The state of *samadhi* as, psychologically viewed, considered as "a mental condition in which the ego is practically dissolved," or a state in which "a withdrawal of the centre of psychic gravity from ego-consciousness" is taking place. *CW*, vol. II, p. 485.

11. Walpola Rahula, *What The Buddha Taught* (New York: Grove Press, 1959), p. 53.

12. The method of amplification is employed by C.G. Jung in order to elaborate and clarify a dream-image by means of directed association and parallels from mythology, folklore, religion, art or literature. According to Jung, "The *amplificatio* is always appropriate when dealing with some dark experience which is so vaguely adumbrated that it must be enlarged and expanded by being set in a psychological context in order to be understood at all. That is why, in analytical psychology, we resort to amplification in the interpretation of dreams, for a dream is too slender a hint to be understood until it is enriched by the stuff of association and analogy and thus amplified to the point of intelligibility." *CW*, vol. 12, p. 277. Hence, Jung's method of amplification allows materials that are obscure and confusing to become clearer and more understandable by permitting them to "speak for themselves."

13. *CW*, vol. 9, part I, p. 275.

14. *CW*, vol. 8, p. 241.

15. The second case of the *Wu Men Kuan*. For an English translation see R.H. Blyth, *Zen and Zen Classics, Vol. Four: Mumonkan* (Tokyo: The Hokuseido Press, 1966), pp. 39-55.

16. *Yu Hsing Ching, Taisho Shinshu Daizokyo*, vols I, II. The Buddha went to the river Ganges and saw people crossing it with boats and rafts. But both the Buddha and his disciples are said to have vanished and stood on the further bank. Then the Buddha preached in the form of these stanzas:

The Buddha is the master of a ship on the ocean.
He is a *dharma* bridge to carry people over to the further port.
He is a palanquin of Tao or a great carrier to carry over all
devas and men.
Also he releases himself from bondage, being able to cross
over to the further shore to ascend to the realm of immortality.
He makes his disciples free from their bondage to enable them
to attain *nirvana*.

The Pali *Maha-parinibbana-sutta*, however has a different verse:

They who cross the ocean drear
Making a solid path across the pools—
Whilst the vain world ties the basket rafts—
These are the wise, these are the saved indeed!

T.W. Rhys Davids, translator, *Buddhist Suttas* (London: Oxford
University Press, 1881), pp. 21-22.
17. *CW*, vol. II, p. 549.
18. *Ibid.*, p. 554.

BUDDHIST EXPERIENCE AS "SELBSTVERWIRKLICHUNG" (Self-Realization)

By Mokusen Miyuki

As a Buddhist priest, I began my own Jungian analysis in order to understand how my experience as a Buddhist related to Western philosophical and religious traditions. In my on-going efforts to integrate these two aspects of my life I offer my current formulation of Jung's basic hypothesis of the individuation process and the Buddhist experience of *satori*.

Buddhism, in my view, is a pragmatic religion and stresses the life-long process of Awakening (bodhi, Enlightenment). In this world of impermanence (*anicca, anitya*),[1] both the objective conditions and the subjective factors are in constant change so that one's Awakening is not a completed, or perfected, state but an ever-changing process which forms a continuum with the impermanence of the interior and exterior world of an individual. The Buddhist concept of Awakening as a process is clearly formulated by the well known Sino-Japanese definition of the term "Buddha": "The one who wakes up to oneself (*tzu-chueh*) and helps others wake up to themselves (*chueh-t'a*) so that the Awakening activity (*chueh-hsing*) goes on to manifest itself infinitely (*ch'iung-man*)[2].

The process of further Awakening is fundamental to an effective confrontation with the "dis-ease" of life (*dukkha, duhkha*), brought about by impermanece. Accordingly, in my recent work, I have asserted the view that Buddhism aims at transformation of

the ego so as to overcome the "dis-ease" of human condition.[4]
Thus understood, Buddhism contradicts the generally prevailing
Western psychological understanding of Buddhism as aiming at
ego-negation or ego-dissolution.

Misconceptions regarding the nature of Buddhism as ego-
negating seem to me to have arisen partly because of the efforts
made by Western Scholars to understand Buddhism through the
utilization of extant philosophical and religious categories in the
West. These Western categories are rooted in a *Weltanschauung* that
is foreign, if not antithetical, to Buddhism. It is my view that C.G.
Jung's Analytical Psychology has provided the West with the first
meaningful psychological avenue to approach Buddhism and
other Asian religious experience.

Jung's perceptive observation and thoughtful statements regarding Asian religions reveal the depth and richness of the insight
afforded him by his empirical and phenomenological methodology.
In my previous writings, especially in "The Ideational Content of
the Buddha's Enlightenment as *Selbstverwirklichung*, or the urge of
the Self to realize itself, can be useful in gaining a better
psychological understanding of Buddhism: namely, Buddhism
aims at transformation of the ego in order to help an individual to
overcome the "dis-ease" of life brought about by impermanence.

Jung uses the term individuation "to denote the process by
which a person becomes a psychological 'in-dividual,' that is, a
separate, indivisible unity or 'whole'." In order to designate the
individuation process, Jung also employs the term *Selbstverwirklichung*.
He states,

> Individuation means becoming a single, homogeneous being,
> and, in so far as "individuality" embraces our innermost, last,
> and incomparable uniqueness, it also implies becoming one's
> own self. We could therefore translate individuation as
> "coming to selfhood" (*zum eigen Selbst werden*, "becoming one's
> own Self") or "self-realization" (*Selbstverwirklichung*, "the Self
> realizing itself").[6]

The German term *Selbstverwirklichung*, which is translated as
"self-realization" in English, indicates psychologically the Self's
innate urge to realize itself. It refers to the self-unfolding process
of "the transpersonal life energy" which "uses human consciousness,
a product of itself, as an instrument for its own self realization."[7]
Therefore, individuation begins with the innate urge of the Self to
realize itself, regardless of the conscious will or external situation.
To become "a single, homogeneous being" is not something the
ego, the center of consciousness, or the empirical man, can create

at will. On the contrary, being driven by the Self's urge, the ego can evolve out of its unconscious conditions. Hence, Jung's concept of *Selbstverwirklichung* can be taken as referring to a "Self-centric" function/condition of the psyche which is supraordinate to the ego-centric function/ condition of the psyche.

The Self is "not only the center but also the whole circumference which embraces both conscious and unconscious."[8] Accordingly, the activation of the Self, the center of the total psyche, causes the ego, the center of consciousness, to function in the service of the Self. As "the smaller circle within the greater circle of the unconscious," or "an island surrounded by the sea" of the unconscious which "yields an endless and self-replenishing abundance of living creatures, a wealth beyond our fathoming,"[9] the ego is constantly conditioned by, and dependent on, the Self as the determining factor for its existence and development. To state it differently, in *Selbstverwirklichung*, the function of the ego can be described, phenomenologically, as "Self-centric," instead of "ego-centric." This "Self-centric" functioning of the ego is not to be confused with the dissolution of the ego. What is "dissolved" in the "Self-centric" function-condition of the psyche, is the "ego-centric" function-condition and not the ego itself. That is, being Self-centered, the ego functions in the service of the Self, the creative matrix of life. The well-known dictum of St. Paul (*Gal.* 2, 20), which Jung refers to frequently in discussing the phenomenology of the Self, can be taken as a classical expression of the "Self-centric" function of the ego, or the ego's functioning in the service of the Self. In this manner, the ego is replenished by assimilating the contents of the unconscious. The ego, thus enriched and strengthened, can become stable enough to integrate even more unconscious material. Psychologically viewed, the Buddhist emphasis on further awakening refers to this constant process of growth and development of the ego. Thus understood, the essential feature of Buddhism does not consist in ego-dissolution but, rather, in ego-enrichment through the integration of the unconscious.

I was born into a Pure Land Jodo Shinshu temple family. My brother is the eighteenth generation of Pure Land priests in our family and I am a second son. I was also ordained as a Pure Land priest, and initially came to this country to serve in a temple while continuing my studies. As you may know, the family tradition is of paramount importance in Japanese culture and my heritage is inextricably bound up with the Pure Land religion. My studies have therefore aimed at understanding and placing this heritage in a wider philosophical-psychological context. My undergraduate work at the University of Tokyo was in Indian philosophy and Buddhism, while my studies in this country began with a reexamination of important Buddhist teachings in the framework of Western philosophy.

While studying Western philosophy I experienced a feeling of intense discomfort with the Western analytical approach and sought an alternate means of understanding my life and family tradition. About this time I began a Jungian analysis and eventually found my way to the Jung Institute in Zurich where for my diploma thesis I studied the Taoist Yoga text the *Secret of the Golden Flower*.[10]

During the course of my training, one of my analysands was Professor T., a Japanese scholar who was well-established in the field of Buddhism. He was sent by the Japanese Ministry of Education in order to study abroad for one and a half years. He was then fifty-two years old and felt quite sure of his direction in life. "As a philosopher," Professor T. told me, "my goal is to get a simultaneous nod between Eastern subjectivity and Western objectivity." What he meant by the word "nod," I presumed, was the synthesis of the spiritual tradition in East and West. As a matter of fact, Professor T. had seriously committed himself to Zen practice since his youth and had been making an extensive study of Western philosophy and religion as well.

Although my analytical experience with Professor T. lasted for only two and a half months, or about twenty-five hours, the depth and wealth of the materials involved, such as dreams, active imaginations, the association experiment, etc., was overwhelming. The analytical experience I had with him has had a permanent influence on my attitude towards understanding unconscious materials. It has also afforded me clear and convincing support for the thesis that the ego's strength and stability are essential for the pursuit of the "genuine self" in Buddhism. Quite a few of his dreams evidently have spoken to this point. Therefore, I would like to utilize some of those dreams which can be taken as a lucid exposition of the function of the ego in *Selbstverwirklichung*, or the self-unfolding process of the Self's urge to realize itself consciously.

The Initial Dream

As Jung points out, the initial dream gives an important hint for the direction of the subsequent analytical process. The first dream Professor T. related to me occurred two and half weeks before our work began:

> My Roshi (from whom he had received much spiritual
> instruction) was about to give me some advice. At that very
> moment, I shouted at him, "K-a-a-a-tsu!" The dream was
> blown off and I awoke with a feeling of regret.

Such a shout, "K-a-a-a-tsu!", in Zen has traditionally been a
gesture to express one's confidence in one's own "genuine self."
As such it is a natural outflow of the "genuine man" within.
Professor T. told me that he experienced real invigorating energy
in this act. Why, then, did he feel regret for the shout when he
awoke? This shout could be understood as not that of the
"genuine man." The ego in this dream seems to have made an
immature response.

It is imperative that the ego be receptive in order to have a
meaningful confrontation with the Self as represented by Professor
T's Zen master. However, in confronting the Self, the ego must be
strong; otherwise, the ego's stability and integrity are threatened
and its disintegration may ensue. Nevertheless, the ego must not
be strong in the sense that it is "rigid," or "inflexible." For, in such
case, the rigid, inflexible ego unreasonably cuts itself off from the
Self, the matrix of life. In other words, what is questioned in this
initial dream is the attitude of the ego in confronting the Self.

An aggressive ego-orientation seems to have been the basic
life-style of Professor T. This observation can be supported by his
earliest recollected childhood experience: One day, Professor T.
was taken to a hospital and saw a doctor giving an injection to a
patient. It was quite exciting for him to discover the fact that an
injection produces a change in the entire body. In remembering his
experience, he said,

> The sharp small needle point penetrates into the body. That
> sharp point, or that point which unites the needle's penetrating
> aggression and the complete passivity of the whole body,
> made me so excited that I felt near ecstasy. Later in childhood,
> even just to think of, or imagine, that sight created in me a
> sort of keen excitement.

In describing the ecstatic excitement he felt connected with the
tiny needle point of aggressiveness and the passiveness of the
body, Professor T. made a grasping gesture with his right hand
while he gazed at an imaginary point before him. Thus, both verbally
and physically, he indicated that the tiny needle "point" represents
for him the "center" uniting the opposites, or the Self. He
explained in this manner that, since early childhood, he had felt an
urgent need to become one with this mysterious "point."

The Second Dream

The second dream, although very short as was the initial dream, indicates also the necessity for ego receptivity in *Selbstverwirklichung*.

> **A meeting is held with the scholar Mr. N. as a leader. There are also many other scholars. Mr. N. is seventy-two years old in the dream. I think to myself that this man is great.**

Professor T. said that for him this dream is quite unexpected because he only once met Mr. N. and did not know him personally. Mr. N. was a famous president of the university at which Professor T. was teaching. After World War II, Mr. N. was influential in guiding the disheartened Japanese who were groping for a way to reconstruct postwar Japan. Mr. N. was also the leader of "Christianity without a church." This Japanese form of Christianity has existed in Japan since around 1910. It was founded by a person named Kanzo Uchimura and about ten to twenty per cent of Japanese Christians are said to follow this form of Christianity. It emphasizes "the church within" as a reaction to what is perceived as the evil tendencies of "institutionalized" Christianity. Hence, the followers believe that their approach is to be considered as the second reformation in Protestantism.

The idea of a "religion without institution" can easily be seen as a derivative of the introverted Japanese Buddhist religion which stresses the significance of the religious awakening or experience, of each individual. For Professor T. this association to Mr. N. in the dream symbolized his pursuing his own way through Zen meditation independent of his Roshi. In addition, his family has traditionally belonged to the Jodo-shinshu. Like the Zen sect, this form of Pure Land Buddhism has been one of the largest Buddhist sects in Japan. It also emphasizes the importance of individual "faith" through the awareness of the unconditional compassion of Amida Buddha. To put it differently, both Zen meditation and the Jodo-shinshu "faith" can be regarded as forerunners of the Japanese Christian idea of "religion without institution," or "the church within." Therefore, for Professor T., Mr. N. represents the embodiment of the creative synthesis of Japanese traditional religiosity and the Western Christian spirit. In this sense, Mr. N. can be taken as an amplification for Professor T.'s goal as a philosopher, i.e., "to get a simultaneous nod between Eastern subjectivity and Western objectivity."

In the dream, many scholars were meeting, with Professor N. as the leader, and Professor T. thought that Mr. N. was great. The respect which Professor T. showed towards Mr. N., or the Self, can be understood as symbolic of the activation of the ego's receptivity in *Selbstverwirklichung*.

The Third Dream

In this dream, the process of activating the receptive function of the psyche is continued further. Four days after the second dream, Professor T. had the following experience:

> As usual, after having done Zen meditation, I went to bed. I gave up trying to sleep and closed my eyes wishing to look into the depths of my being. While I was falling into a doze, my latent consciousness shouted, "K-city!" and I suddenly came back to consciousness. After a short while, I went back to sleep again.

K-city is the hometown of Professor T. He associated it with the depth of the psyche, or his "genuine home." "This genuine home, however," he said,

> does not usually exist in my consciousness. It is experienced like heavenly music in the state of *samadhi* concentration, or occasionally, in the state of ordinary consciousness... Since I consciously wished to look into the depths of my being, my hometown, "K", which has been in my latent consciousness, must have been activated in conjunction with the "genuine home" or the depth of my psyche.

Then, he added, "But, this kind of interpretation does not contribute anything to the promotion of my Zen practice. Dream analysis thus seems meaningless to me!"

For Professor T., The depth of the psyche, or the unconscious, is the "genuine home" of the creative matrix. Yet, his additional remarks reveal intellectual aggressiveness which often ends up with a mere interpretation. A rational interpretation cuts off the inner wealth of the unconscious. In contrast to the initial dream in which the ego acted aggressively to the Self, in this dream the ego takes a more receptive attitude towards the unconscious. As stated in his remarks, what Professor T. needed was not an interpretation but an event or an experience of creative depth so that he could appreciate his "genuine man." This direction towards a meaningful experience of the unconscious took place in the subsequent dreams.

After the third dream, Professor T. had no dreams for about a

week. He deplored that, saying, "Dreams have abandoned me!"
Then, the fourth dream came.

The Fourth Dream

The dream begins with my feeling deeply how difficult *sumo*
wrestling is. There are three *yokozuna* champions: the veteran,
the up-coming one, and myself who was just promoted to the
yokozuna rank. Both the veteran and the up-coming one have
been in low spirits these days. Now my turn to wrestle has
come. I stamp in high spirits on the ring's edge in a warm-up. I
do feel very refreshed. As soon as I stand up, I try to push my
opponent off. With the movement of my hands to push him
off, I woke up. My opponent was the veteran *yokozuna*.

Sumo-wrestling has been a traditional Japanese national sport as
well as a professional show. Originally, however, the *sumo*-match
had a close relationship to religious activity in the Shinto religion.
Even today, in a certain district, an amateur *sumo*-match at the
matsuri-festival is dedicated to the *kami*, or divinity, of the shrine. In
the *sumo*-match, the entire person of the *sumo*-wrestler is "purified"
in both body and mind so as to be prepared for the presence of the
divinity. Therefore, psychologically speaking, the *sumo*-match symbolizes the complete submission, or sacrifice, of the total being to
the divine being, or the Self.

Professor T. likes watching *sumo*-wrestling, especially the veterans'
matches, which are filled with the "vital puff." He said,

The veterans' "vital puff" is of a similar quality to the
breathing of Zen meditation. I am now feeling the difficulty of
getting through the last point into Great *Nirvana*. I believe the
way to *Nirvana* consists in Zen sitting. . . My total being, my
body, my mind are ultimately converging into that one point.
That point is of the utmost difficulty to penetrate.

It should be noted that the ego in this fourth dream is filled with
the "vital puff." Hence the veteran *yokozuna*, who represents
Professor T.'s former "genuine self," must have been outgrown,
pushed off to the outside of the ring, although the dream does not
relate this to us. An open-ended dream, as Jung maintains, should
be concluded in real life. The image of the ego filled with the "vital
puff" can be taken as the ego functioning in the service of the Self.
That is, in *Selbstverwirklichung*, the ego begins to function in a
"self-centric" way or in perfect unison with the "Self-centric"
psychic condition.

Professor T's last remarks on this dream were again skeptical and critical of his interpretation. He stated,

> I understand that this dream is related to the actual difficulty I have getting through the last point into the *Great Nirvana*. Beyond this, I cannot see any 'meaning'. Who is the *Yokozuna*? He is simply the last rank achieved among *sumo*-wrestlers. On what ground, can I be related to the *yokozuna* in my real life? Even if I and the *yokozuna* were related and went on to interpret this dream, this interpretation has no significant bearing on my major concern. Such an interpretation is merely worldy and non-religious.

Thus, as it was before in case of the third dream, Professor T. became all the more aware of Zen meditation as the essential method for realizing his objective, i.e., the "genuine home," of the Great *Nirvana*, or the "nod" of a simultaneous realization of Eastern subjectivity and Western objectivity.

The Fifth Dream

Professor T.'s search for the "last point" to penetrate into *Nirvana* continues even in his dreams:

> In this dream, I am searching for the subject who is now dreaming. While searching for it, I found the surface of the dream covered with something like ice (yet not cold) and a board (yet half-transparent) which was rather thick and flat. While I am thinking that I cannot know the content of the dream any longer, I become half-awakened.

Professor T., for the first time, made very positive remarks about his dreams. He said, "In the state of half-sleeping, I found myself pleased for making efforts to get closer to the depth of the psyche." Then, he stated, "My goal as a philosopher is to realize a simultaneous nod between Eastern subjectivity and Western objectivity. It is a far distance to get there, yet I feel that I have made a step ahead towards it." His additional remarks on his experiences after this dream are quite revealing in the light of the ego's function in *Selbstverwirklichung*. He wrote:

> It has been several hours since I had this dream. During these hours, the wind, which transcends the world and which comes through the depths of the psyche, has been blowing. It comes from the depth through the subconscious to consciousness, to my ego and to my body. I am simultaneously in and out of *Zen samadhi*. This wind will stop when time comes.

It seems that Professor T. experienced the "genuine home" of the creative unconscious in his awakened state as the result of his dream efforts to search for the dreaming subject. As he comments, what took place was a simultaneous act of subjectivity or dreaming and objectivity of searching for the dreaming subject. His realization that "I cannot know the content of the dream any longer" can be taken as the death of the ego's aggressive attitude, which is followed by the birth of ego receptivity in *Selbstverwirklichung*. The ego, being thus passive and receptive, now experiences the unity of the total being penetrated by the wind, or creative energy, coming up from the "genuine home" of the matrix of life. This is the state of being in which the last point into *Nirvana* was penetrated and in which, accordingly, the joy of the genuine breath of creative life energy wells up. The invigorating shout to the Zen master, or the "vital puff" of the *yokozuna* wrestler, has now become a living reality which he describes as being "simultaneously in and out of *Zen-samadhi*."

The state of being which Professor T. described as being "simultaneously in and out of *Zen-samadhi*" occured to him from time to time. "It is experienced," as he stated while discussing the third dream, "like heavenly music in the state of *samadhi* concentration, or occasionally, in the state of ordinary consciousness." Sometimes, he said, the joy welling up from the "genuine home" continued for several days. One of these unforgettable experiences of the genuine being took place when Professor T. was a young university student.

He was seriously struggling with the unsolvable existential problems of life. His knowledge and his Zen practice did not help him to cope with his spiritual agony and suffering. He experienced himself as a "suffering chaos" day after day, night after night. On one of those days, towards evening, a sudden "explosion" of the "suffering chaos" into the living eternity of joy took place when he was reading a Buddhist text in the library. He said,

> The bag of that chaos exploded all of a sudden. At that very moment, my spiritual agony and suffering were blown off into empty space (*koku*). Myself, the world, everything became one. Nothing whatsoever was there. No heaven, no earth, no myself, except only 'the living, naked, empty space'. It was the clear manifestation of the genuine self. It was the moment of living truth pulsating in eternity. After a short while, I realized that it was the ultimate goal now completed.
>
> This realization was turned into a welling joy from the bottom of my being and my whole body was penetrated by a whirling vortex of joy. I could not recall how I was able to get home. For the following ten days or so, I experienced a life

totally fulfilled from the bottom of my being. I felt the interpenetration of the body and the mind, as if they mirrored each other in a double mirror.

The Last Dream

As mentioned previously, Professor T. ended his analysis with me after two and half months. However, the objective psyche carried on the process and sought to fulfill his open-ended dream of the *sumo* match. After another two months had passed, he wrote a letter and shared with me the following dream experience:

> We were digging a tunnel with my teacher, who was the authority in this field of tunnel digging. Many people were under our command. The trial digging was successful. The teacher insisted, "With the agreement of theory and practice like this, we will without fail succeed." But I disagreed, saying "It's wrong! No tunnel can be dug in such a manner. The agreement of theory and practice is only a painted rice cake [impractical], so that we should theorize while practicing and practice while theorizing. This is the true way (*michi*). Your method is wrong and will without a doubt fail." The teacher insisted on the correctness of his view and held his opinion with confidence. His attitude reminded me of the people in Meiji era [1868-1912]. I repeatedly and earnestly explained that his view was wrong and that his method was so dangerous that he must stop. But he believed firmly that his way was right and began to dig the tunnel by himself, saying that he would go his own way. We helped him and followed him. The work had progressed nicely and seemed to end with a success. But, soon, the upper foundation of the place where the teacher was working began to shake. "Dangerous! Let's go out quickly!" Calling to each other, we ran for our lives to the outside through the rising smoke around us. Fortunately, we were all safe; but we could not rescue our teacher. A fire started inside the tunnel, burning rapidly. Thus, the teacher died for his conviction.
>   A senior friend of the teacher, who is also a type of Meiji character and who always wore *Haorio* and *Hakama* [Japanese traditional full dress], said to us with tears: "Why haven't you shared your teacher's lot!" I responded, saying, "No, it is not the way! I had pointed out the mistake of my teacher's method and insisted on not continuing. But, he went on by himself. Our way is not to share our lot with him, but to dig the tunnel through!" While saying this, I felt as if my body became the tunnel itself. My whole body became rigid, confonting my own way (*michi*) which I must follow.

I awoke from this dream with a strange feeling. The following words flashed in my mind:

> The dream is merely the shadow of human life. Those who
> inquire into the shadow will perish with the shadow. We must
> not chase the shadow. Turn to the substance of the shadow.
> Become that reality to go on as that reality. That is the White
> Path!
>   I came to realize that this is *the real substance* (*jittai*) *of faith* (*shin*)
> for the new age. The real substance is that which I have been
> seeking for a long time, namely *the thing* (*mono*) itself, the
> subjectivity itself, or the karma (*go*) itself!" (Italics are his.)

Phenomenologically, this dream speaks to Professor T.'s realization of his objective: namely, getting through "the last point into the Great *Nirvana*," or the point into which his whole being, body and mind, ultimately converges. To get through this "last point" also would satisfy his academic ambition for the achievement of "a simultaneous nod between Eastern subjectivity and Western objectivity."

The image of the teacher, for Japanese of Professor T's age, overlaps with that of the guru who guides the student in his spiritual journey. In this sense, Professor T.'s teacher was quite successful in helping him to become a "teacher" who succeeded in his objective, namely to dig the tunnel. Hence, the death of the teacher represents the integration of the teacher's way, or *tao*, to become a genuine individual. Since the people of the Meiji era emphasized the importance of the "Japanese spirit" in integrating Western science and technology, the death of Professor T.'s new teacher, an embodiment of this era, symbolizes the death of his orientation. To use Professor T.'s dream expression, this Meiji orientation of pursuing the way, or *tao*, which stresses the agreement of theory and practice, is "wrong," "dangerous," hence, "to be stopped."

The agreement of theory and practice was upheld by the Neoconfucian teacher/scholar Wang Yang-ming (1472-1529) and his followers in the Far East in terms of *chin-hsing ho-i*, or "the unity of theory and practice." Wang Yang-ming was known as a practitioner of *ching-tso* (meditative sitting) which he considered as the means to realize his doctrine. His Neo-confucianism had been influential in Japan and greatly contributed to the formation of the character of the Meiji Japanese. Therefore, the death of Professor T.'s teacher also symbolized for him the birth of a new way, or *tao*, which Professor T. designated as "*the real substance of faith* for the new age," "the thing itself, the subjectivity itself, or karma itself."

The new tao, which is symbolically expressed by these synonyms, is quite well represented by Professors T.'s experience of becoming the tunnel itself, the very tunnel through which he must dig. For him, theory and practice form a continuum. The application of theory to practice and the agreement of the two are no longer his way. Theory and practice are not two but a unitary whole which Professor T. experiences in the act of his digging the tunnel as his path constantly unfolding itself. In the act of digging ("karma itself"), the two, the digger ("the subjectively itself") and that which is dug ("the *thing* itself") are dynamically united as a living whole.

This experience is what Professor T. termed as the life of "a simultaneous nod between Eastern subjectivity and Western objectivity." Furthermore, Professor T.'s total being is experienced as the tunnel, or that axial point into which his total being ultimately converges to get through into the Great *Nirvana*.

Psychologically viewed, the ego (the digger) is integrated through its "ego-centric" act of digging, into the urge of the Self to realize itself. This is to say, the ego functions in the service of, and in perfect unison with, the "Self-centric" function/condition of the creative psyche, which Professor T. associated with the White Path.[11] This observation can be supported by his symbolic experience of being simultaneously the digger and that which is dug. It was Shinran (1173-1262), the founder of the Jodo-shinshu, who appreciated the White Path. His total existence was illuminated by the "faith" (*shin-jin*) which is given by Amida Buddha, or the Self. Therefore, Professor T.'s unique realization of his dream experience as the White Path is to be understood as an expression of his family tradition.

The Buddhist experience which Professor T. relates to us effectively supports the view that Buddhism is a pragmatic religion and stresses the life-long process of awakening. Professor T.'s repeated experiences of the archetype of the Self and his insightful remarks reveal that the Buddhist way of living can be understood as the process of individuation which Jung also designated as "becoming one's own Self" (*zum eigen Selbst werden*) as well as "the Self realizing itself" (*Selbstverwirklichung*). Professor T.'s experience provides an Eastern example of the individuation process in which the constant renewal and growth of the ego takes place in the context of *Selbstverwirklichung*. His ego-oriented academic goal of synthesizing Eastern subjectivity and Western objectivity was integrated in his unique version of the White Path in which the ego was constantly replenished through its receptive attitude in order to function in the service of the urge of the Self realizing itself.

FOOTNOTES

1. The first word in the parenthesis is Pali, and the second Sanskrit.

2. This definition of the term "Buddha" is given by Hui-yaun (523-592 A.D.) in his famous treatise, *Ta-cheng i-chang* (The Essentials of Mahayana Doctrine), in Taisho Vol. 44 no. 1851, p. 864.

3. For a detailed discussion of "dis-ease" see Mokusen Miyuki," Living with *Duhka*, in *East/West Culture: Religious Motivations for Behavior* (Santa Barbara: Educational Futures, International, 1977), pp. 57-64.

4. M. Miyuki, "A Jungian Approach to the Pure Land Practice of *Nien-fo*," in *The Journal of Analytical Psychology* Vol. 25, no. 3 (July 1980), pp. 265-274; *"Selbstverwirklichung"* in the *Ten Oxherding Pictures"* (A paper presented at the Eighth International Congres of International Association for Analytical Psychology, San Francisco, September 1980); "The Ideational Content of the Buddha's Enlightenment as *Selbstverwirklichung"* (A paper for the anthology of *Buddhist and Western Psychology*, edited by Nathan Katz. All of these as well as the article in Note 3 are represented in this volume.

5. C.G. Jung, "Conscious, Unconscious, and Individuation," in *The Archetypes and the Collective Unconscious*. The Collected Works of C.G. Jung, Vol. 9, i, par. 275., hereafter known as *CW*.

6. C.G. Jung, *Two Essays on Analytical Psychology. CW*, Vol. 7, par. 266.

7. E.F. Edinger, *Ego and Archetype* (Baltimore, Maryland: Penguin Books Inc., 1973), p. 104.

8. C.G. Jung, *Psychology and Alchemy. CW*, Vol. 12. par. 44.

9. C.G. Jung, *The Practice of Psychotherapy. CW*, Vol. 16, par. 366.

10. M. Miyuki, *Kreisen des Lichtes: die Erfahrung der goldene Blute.* Weilheim, Otto Wilhelm Verlag. (A translation of a diploma thesis for the C.G. Jung Institute, Zurich, entitled *The Secret of the Golden Flower: Studies and Translation.*)

11. For a detailed discussion on the White Path, see M. Miyuki, "A Jungian Approach to the Pure Land Practice of *Nien-fo.*"

AFTERWORD
By J. Marvin Spiegelman

When I completed my commentary on the Ox-herding Pictures (see above), I felt a pleasant sense of fulfilling a long desired goal which was both an obligation and a joy, but I also experienced a mild sense of guilt. A voice within me said, "Yes, you have met the need to write a commentary on the Ox-herding pictures and have done so in an adequate Jungian fashion, but all your analogies have been Christian. Jesus is the one to compare with Buddha, apparently. Where is your own tradition, Judaism, and where are the other paths to the divine which can be compared with the Buddhistic view from a psychological angle?" This gnawing question made me remember that someone had written a book on Zen and Hasidism, but one I had never read. I therefore resolved to get that book and to write another chapter which would include Judaism, particularly Jewish mysticism, and Islam, particularly the Sufi tradition, with a Jungian view-point. On summer holiday, therefore, I took along that book on *Zen and Hasidism*, compiled by Haifetz (1978) as well as two books of Sufi (Burkhardt 1959; Shah 1970) another on fundamental *Mitnagdim* Judaism (Soloveitchik 1983) and my old copy of the *Koran*.

I read the foregoing books with pleasure and appreciation and was given to considerable reflection. When it came to writing the desired comparison, however, my typewriter failed me. When I asked this same voice how it was that nothing appeared to fulfill its request, a silence greeted me. More reflection, however, reminded me that it was similar when I tried to bring my thoughts on the Ox-herding pictures to fruition before the time was right. Since it took more than twenty years for that to happen, would it take as long to produce another commentary with Judaism and Islam? The voice said no, it would not take so long, but that

185

another book was involved, and that would take time and devotion. That book, something like Judaism and Jungian Psychology, or Judaism, Islam and Jungian Psychology, as well as another on Jungian Psychology and Christianity, are, therefore, in the works. I have since discovered that the latter topic already has its more recent adherents (e.g. *The Illness That We Are: A Jungian Critique of Christianity*, by John P. Dourley), and that the former topic will require considerably more reading and thought. (Since writing the foregoing, my publisher has suddenly asked me to write a chapter on Jungian Psychology and Judaism for another book he is preparing. Such meaningful coincidences -- synchronicities as Jung called them -- make one feel that one is, indeed, on the right track or in harmony with the energies of the time.)

The reason that I mention these reflections and plans in this context is only to introduce a summary topic on what it means to have a psychological view of religion at all! Somewhere, there is a guilt involved. There is a separation or distancing -- however well-intentioned or loving -- from the religion or tradition of one's birth, up-bringing or ancestry that comes with the shift to the point of view of the psychologist. The danger of reductionism -- so that, for example, the partaking of the Eucharist in the Mass is just a "symbol" or that the Law in Judaism is merely a "pattern of behavior" -- is only too obvious to those of us who have a deep respect and love for both sides of the formula, "psychology and religion." Indeed, some of us insist upon the statement of "Psychology *and* Religion" rather than "psychology *of* religion" since it is only a short and terrifyingly destructive step to reverse the formula and have a "religion of psychology." The latter might be called a religion of science, or scientism. That attitude leaves one with the worst of the sins against the numinous, that of luke-warmness, neglect or indifference. Scientism, like atheism, can be redeemed by passionate adherence, which then makes it a faith like any other. The Lord seems to forgive rejection as long as He/She receives attention.

How, then, is one to achieve forgiveness for this guilt of distantiation provided by applying a psychological point-of-view? I think that this becomes possible by dissolving the one-sidedness of objectivity in subjectivity. One must deepen the affective dimension of appreciation and worship without losing the achievements of greater understanding. My models for such an attitude are in the great book of the Dutch Protestant theologian, Gerhard van der Leeuw, *Religion in Essence and Manifestation* (1938) and that of the aforementioned Rabbinical scholar, Joseph B. Soloveitchik. The former, after a long, profound and complete exposition of every type of religious experience and belief system, with a scholarly and appreciative rendering behind his phenomenological view-point, concludes his book with the statement that the scholar must now retreat and become the man who bows, at the altar, to the God of his fathers and his own existence. Rabbi Soloveitchik, similarly, after a careful and precise rendering of the life of the man of God who thoughtfully and lovingly attends to the patterns of existence handed down by Tora and Tradition, now modestly reduces the significance of his contribution and begs forgiveness for any harm that he might have unintentionally done. Such is the model of the man of God, who has performed the *sacrificium intellectus* in the most satisfying way, namely used his intellectual capacities with both maximum criticism and devotion. Such are the ones who, like Plato, make reason the slave of the passions, bow before the numinous, and do not succumb to the hybris so tantalizingly but foolishly represented by the fallen angels. The redemption of such fallen but "progressive" spirits is to do just what our models have done, namely to turn their intellects toward service of the divine. So, then, I believe, is the guilt of objectivity and distantiation recompensed by devotion.

This, it seems to me, is just what Jung did in his life - long work. In his general writing, he maintained a strict scientific attitude, but always with appreciation and honor to the psychological material at hand. Nor did he ever abandon the religion of his birth and ancestry, however far afield might he go and however broad his definition and inclusion of contents inimical to the official standards of faith at the time. Thus, then, was he rewarded in later life by the experience, as he beautifully describes in his autobiography, *Memories, Dreams, Reflections,* (1961) of successive nights of rapture, encompassing the chief imagery and highest experience of Greek Polytheism, Judaism and Christianity.

None of us who have read those accounts of his dreams can remain unmoved by the sincerity and profundity of his experience of these three religions. He was both "within" them and "outside" of them in that he was ecumenical in the deepest sense of the word. He was multiply-connected and also psychological. It is no surprise, therefore, when we hear of other dreams of Jung which are clearly Hindu, Buddhist, or have a flavor of Islam, as well as many with alchemical, gnostic and pagan themes. I would think that Jung was perhaps the first of the "modern men" who, having "lost his soul," found it by dint of his own individual experience, and still kept his links with the religions of the past. Jung preferred the etymology of "religio" as a "careful observation of the numinous," yet his life-long attitude, it seems to me, embraced that other origin of the word as "linking back." Jung linked fully with the past, historically and respectfully.

What does this mean for us in terms of our present investigation? I think it gives a hint as to how we can approach such topics as psychology and religion in the modern day. Every world religion, including Buddhism, seems to develop its branches of fundamentalism, traditionalism, mysticism, freedom for individuality and the converse. This variety mirrors the different aspects of our own souls. Jungian psychology, I believe, has given us a working attitude toward this variety, by being receptive to whatever the psyche brings forth, individually or collectively ("let the soul speak for itself" said Tertullian). This attitude allows us to understand that all the works of religion have been the voice of the soul in the past.

The dream and fantasy of my youth (recounted in East and West: A Personal Statement) -- in which the three wise men or kings who were now coming to visit a new divine child, were a Jewish Rabbi, a Christian Priest, and a Buddhist Priest -- is similar in spirit, if not in depth, to the ecumenical experience of Jung. This leads me to believe that something new is emerging from the psyche, another way of approaching the numinous. This newer experience of the divine is to be found in a reconciliation among the religions of the world and their ability to worship and connect with a new content. I think that this content, which independently emerged both in Jung and in others, is a kind of psycho-religious attitude, if one can use such a word. The qualities of this attitude are: the divine transcends us all; there are many paths to it, all of which have truth, or are part of a whole; all paths are worthy, none better than others; none need be transcended; all religions find their origin in the nature of the soul itself and how the divine manifests therein. This is surely a Hindu view, a Buddhist view, a Jewish view, a Christian view, but only for some sects or branches of each one. The psychological view is a unifying one, I think, but hard come by for the reasons (guilt) that I mention at the outset.

I have elsewhere described how, in practice, the union of a psychological and a religious view-point is, in fact, rather rare (Psychotherapy and the Clergy: Fifty Years Later, 1984). The problem seems to be in the relativization of the ego, a word used by Jung and resting also in the consciousness-shaking discoveries of Albert Einstein. It refers to those experiences of the person who not only discovers that forces larger than himself reside in his own soul, but ultimately, with long work, finds that his own center of existence shifts to that internal paradoxical point and circumference which both encompasses him and is at his core. It is the "God within," the "God without," and the "God among." The experience itself seems to be fairly rare, and thus, I have found, even clergy and editors of religious journals bridle at the word "relativization."

This same "relativization," however, is at the heart of Buddhism, as is shown in the Zen Ox-herding pictures, and it is precisely at this point that Buddhism and Jungian psychology coalesce. It may have been a foolish blending of concepts when I suggested that those pictures illustrate not only the path to "Enlightenment" but also to Jung's "Individuation," as well. There are, of course, differences between the concepts, but the central experience which is being portrayed -- the relativization of the ego -- is that which encompasses both.

From my own dream of long ago, I would think that this would be the chief "gift" that the Buddhist priest (in my psyche at least) would be bringing to the new divine child. The central gifts given by the Christian priest, I would think, would be the God-man experience, fundamentally the humanization of God and the divinization of man. The Jewish rabbi's gift, for me, would be the fundamental experience of the divine itself, within and without, alone and in community, bound and free, eternally submitting to divine law and eternally engaging the Other in dialogue.

Such gifts to the divine child of the emerging "ecumenization" of mankind seem very great indeed. We (I) do not yet know what the gifts of the divine child to us will be, in turn, but I think that one of them is a psychological point of view, one that permits us to experience the divine from multiple vantage points and allows reflection and questioning, as well. Part of that gift has already come through Jung's work, I think, but the fact that I had my dream long before knowing of Jung's dreams or visions suggests that the content is emerging from the unconscious itself in many people. Consonant with the world's condition at this time, there seems to be more expectation or desire that the new divine child, "savior," is to appear outside ourselves rather than inside. Thus there is the awaited Messiah, Second Coming, the fullfillment of prophecy, and in a more modern vein, the sense that our earth will encounter (or has already) consciousness from other planets or stars. They are all probably right, but it is Jung's -- and Buddhism's -- gift to us to look for that emergence from within our own souls. So, we all will have a lot to do with ourselves until that outer Buddha, Christ, Messiah, appears. God willing, it will be synchronistic. It is noted in Jewish lore, that when every Jew observes Shabbat, the Messiah will appear. To extrapolate, when all of us are in tune with the Divine Presence, HE/SHE/IT will manifest among us all.

REFERENCES

Burckhardt, Titus, *An Introduction to Sufi Doctrine*, Sh. Muhammad Ashraf, Lahore, Pakistan, 1959. 155 pp.

Dourley, John P., *The Illness That We Are: A Jungian Critique of Christianity*. Inner City Books, Toronto, 1984.

Haifetz, Harold, ed., *Zen & Hasidism*. The Theosophical Publishing House, Wheaton, Illinois. 1978. 242 pp.

Jung, C.G., *Memories, Dreams, Reflections*. Random House, New York, 1961. 398 pp.

The Koran, translated by E.H. Palmer, Oxford University Press, London, 1928.

Leeuw, Gerhard van der, *Religion in Essence and Manifestation*. George Allen & Unwin, London, 1938. 710 pp.

Shah, Idries, *Tales of the Dervishes*. E.P. Dutton & Co,, New York, 1970. 222 pp.

Soloveitchik, Joseph B., *Halakhic Man*. Jewish Publication Society of America, Philadelphia, 1983. 164 pp.

Spiegelman, J. Marvin. "Psychotherapy and the Clergy: Fifty Years Later." *Journal of Religion and Health, 1984; Vol. 23, #11, pp. 19-32.*